ORCHIDS
CARE AND
CULTIVATION

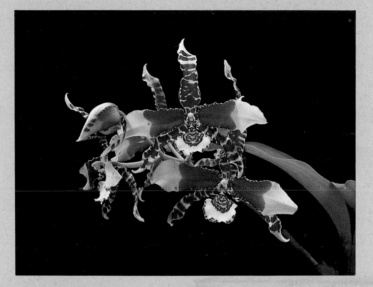

GÉRALD LEROY-TERQUEM & JEAN PARISOT

ORCHIDS
CARE AND
CULTIVATION

Foreword by
Maurice Lecoufle

CASSELL

Osmoglossum pulchellum

page 1: *Rossioglossum grande*
page 2: *Zygopetalum* blackii 'Negus', AM/RHS

Cassell Publishers Limited
Villiers House, 41/47 Strand
London WC2N5JE

First published in the United Kingdom 1991
This edition 1993, reprinted 1994
English text © Cassell Publishers Ltd. 1991
Original edition *Comment choisir et entretenir vos orchidées* Copyright ©
BORDAS, Paris 1989

British Library Cataloguing in Publication Data

Leroy-Terquem, Gérald
    Orchids.
    I. Orchids
    I. Title   II. Parisot, Jean III. [Comment choisir et
entretenir vos orchidées. *English*]
    584.15
ISBN 0-304-34329-3

Distributed in the United States by
Sterling Publishing Co. Inc
387 Park Avenue South, New York, N.Y. 10016-8810

Distributed in Australia by
Capricorn Link (Australia) Pty Ltd
2/13 Carrington Road. Castle Hill, N S W 2154

English translation by John Gilbert
Line drawings by Sylvie Chrétien
Photographs by Gérald Leroy-Terquem and
National Museum of Natural History, Paris (pp. 9, 11, 12, 13, 14, 16, 30, 34
French Horticultural Society (p. 10)
Archives INRA (p. 15)

Typeset by August Filmsetting, Haydock, St Helens

Printed and bound by New Interlitho, Milan

Contents

5

Foreword

Laeliocattleya Stradivarius

I GREW UP WITH ORCHIDS. Their colours thrilled me, they seemed to speak to me... and I am certain it was their shimmering contrasts and infinite range of tones that first inspired my love, aroused my interest and eventually persuaded me to cultivate them. I remember my feelings the first time I saw the glorious red flush of the sky as the sun set over an island in the Pacific. If only one could recapture such a beautiful, dazzling colour.... . Imagine my delight when, much later, in crossing a pink *Phalaenopsis* with a yellow one, I obtained an orchid of that very red hue which had so moved me years earlier.

It is scarcely possible to talk about orchids without mentioning their scent, sometimes quite ravishing yet not universally appreciated... delighting some, repelling others. Whereas the colours endure, the scents, with the purely functional purpose of attracting insects at the most favourable moments of day and night, are often so fleeting that at other times it is hardly possible to catch a trace of them.

Contrary to what is usually said, and despite the doubts often expressed, the orchid is the indoor plant *par excellence*; indeed no other affords so much satisfaction and pleasure. It is not uncommon for it to continue flowering for five or six weeks, while the *Phalaenopsis* species and certain *Cattleya* bloom for even longer. All that is needed is a window-sill, some auxiliary electric lighting and a few elementary precautions, as described in this book, to obtain truly spectacular results.

A passion for orchids takes you into a complex and boundless world where you are always making new discoveries. . . . Indeed, it would take more than a lifetime to explore and get to know the 25,000–30,000 species found in nature. But in this world of exotic orchids there is also the added excitement of improving species by cross-breeding, of creating new hybrids and thus new forms and colours.

Now that plants can be raised from seed and propagated from meristems, orchids are no longer as rare and difficult to grow as they were at the beginning of the present century. The majority are replaceable and can be grown without serious risks and problems.

As in so many fields of endeavour, trial and error is a determining factor in the cultivation of orchids. This book, designed for all lovers of these plants, describes the subtle interactions to which orchids are subjected when removed from their natural surroundings and assesses their basic requirements.

It is a great pleasure for me to write a foreword to a book which both reveals these flowers in all their magnificence and deals so thoroughly with the essential techniques for growing them. M. Jean Parisot and Dr Gérald Leroy-Terquem have brought all their experience and enthusiasm to a remarkable text that manages to be both factual and lyrical; and it is worthily supplemented by Dr Leroy-Terquem's exceptional photographs. From rare tropical orchids to hybrid varieties of the most astonishing beauty and originality, virtually every aspect of this fabulous realm is offered here for our instruction and delight.

Obviously this is a practical book but it is also one to browse through simply for pleasure, calculated to arouse that shiver of excitement that is familiar to every true lover of orchids.

MAURICE LECOUFLE

Introduction

Growing naturally in most subtropical regions, *Vanilla* is a very primitive orchid, the origins of which date back 120 million years. (Engraving by Hooker, early nineteenth century.)

THE ORCHIDS MAKE up one of the biggest families of flowering plants, yet also one of the most highly evolved. According to current estimations, there are some 730 genera and 25,000 species in existence. Extremely diversified, they are to be found in virtually all regions around the world, except for deserts. So they flourish in the Alps as well as in the tropics, near the polar circles and, although rarely, in the suburbs of certain cities of western Europe.

Theophrastus, around 300 BC, was the first to record the resemblance of the tubercles of certain Mediterranean species to a pair of testicles. Almost certainly he was not the first to notice this similarity, but history does not record the author of the name *Orchis* (Greek *orkhis*, testicle), which is still used today for the European genus, and which was to originate the name of the entire family.

Introduction of tropical orchids to Europe

It was not until the sixteenth century that the first exotic orchids found their way to Europe, thanks to exploration, expanding trade and religious missions. Botanists, of course, took an immediate interest in these plants, even though the specimens which reached them were often in a miserable state.

In 1552, vanilla was mentioned for the first time in Western literature when it was listed in the *Badianus* manuscript, the earliest known study of South American flora. This plant, which is certainly the most commercialized of all orchids, had been introduced in the form of pods or beans to the European market several decades beforehand, in 1510.

In 1688, John Ray, in his *Historia Plantarum*, described *Disa uniflora*, a most beautiful orchid from the Cape of Good Hope, but not sufficiently striking to draw from him the faintest lyrical outburst, merely the laconic definition: 'African orchid, unusual flower, herbaceous'.

The spread of exploration, particularly on the continent of Asia towards the end of the seventeenth century, enabled botanists to discover new species, such as those of the genus *Dendrobium*. Apart from describing them in some detail, those who found such species were concerned principally to catalogue their discoveries and to draw up lists of plants, often in somewhat debatable groups. Even so, this was a necessary prerequisite to more elaborate observations and studies which culminated, in 1735, in the first coherent system of plant identification and classification: the Linnaean system. This established the binomial description of living organisms (generic name followed by specific name) and their grouping in families. Moreover, Linnaeus proposed a highly original method of classification based, among other things, upon the structure of the sexual organs (pistil and stamen). But the Linnaean system, in fact, went far beyond mere names and classifications, its revolutionary importance consisting in the fact that it revealed – or would later reveal – the major lines of development of living beings and the laws of evolution. It opened the way for Darwin who, it is interesting to note, spent much of his time observing orchids and their method of pollination.

Darwin's work, entitled *The Various Contrivances by which Orchids Are Fertilized by Insects*, published in 1862, made the first essential contribution to the understanding of the strategies which orchids, thanks to insects, employ to ensure cross-pollination. Darwin emphasized, and was the first botanist to do so, that each species of orchid was closely dependent on a specific type of insect to carry out its pollination.

Disa uniflora. A difficult species to cultivate, *Disa uniflora* is one of the loveliest orchids from South Africa.

One of the most famous examples of this is the Madagascan orchid *Angraecum sequipedale*. The rear part of the lip of this species is modified: it is a hollow spur measuring some 12 in (30 cm), of which only the last 4 in (10 cm) secretes nectar. Based on such observations, Darwin boldly concluded that this structure was associated with the presence, in the plant's natural environment, of an insect furnished with a proboscis of equivalent length which effects pollination after the insect is gorged with nectar. In view of the fact that the fauna of Madagascar was little known at that time, such an assertion appeared to defy all reason. Yet forty years later entomologists on the island discovered a huge moth of the sphinx family with an extremely long proboscis; when extended, this could reach to the base of the *Angraecum* spur. As a tribute to Darwin and his far-sightedness, the moth was given a double specific name, *Xanthopan morgani praedicta*.

The very first tropical orchid to be cultivated in Europe was *Brassavola nodosa*, imported into the Netherlands around the end of the seventeenth century. The second was probably *Bletia verecunda*, discovered in the Bahamas and sent back to Peter Collinson in England in 1731; in the summer of the following year the horticulturalist and collector of rare plants, Sir Charles Wager, succeeded in getting it to flower. These two successes do not appear to have been emulated, for in 1768, the second edition of Miller's *Gardener's Dictionary* had this to say about *Epidendrum* (then the name given to all tropical orchids): 'As the plants cannot, by any art yet known, be cultivated in the ground, it would be to little purpose the enumerating of them here; though could the plants be brought to thrive by culture, many of them produce very fine flowers of uncommon forms.'

Some years later, Dr John Fothergill brought back from China several orchids, including *Phaius grandifolius* (introduced as *Limodorum tankervilleae* or *Bletia tankervilleae*, changed to *Phaius tankervilleae* in 1856) and *Cymbidium ensifolium*; from 1778 he grew these plants quite successfully and apparently managed to keep them alive for several years. In 1787 an *Epidendrum cochleatum* flowered at the Royal Botanic Gardens, Kew, soon followed by an *Epidendrum fragrans*. Over the next seven years some fifteen *Epidendrum* species were grown at Kew: raised under strong heat, they just about survived. But one definite step forward had been taken: these orchids were not potted in ordinary soil but in a substrate consisting of decomposed bark.

These earliest epiphytic orchids came from the West Indies and were brought back, mainly to England, by travellers or captains of merchant ships who were not concerned with making botanical or climatic observations during their travels. Virtually nothing, therefore, was understood of the

Angraecum sesquipedale became famous as a result of Darwin's work. (Engraving by Aubert du Petit-Thouars, 1822.)

Orch. Afr o *reg.* bis 17.   67

Dolichangis   *Angræcum sesquipedale*

conditions and particular requirements for growing these plants and keeping them healthy. Little more was known than that they grew on trees and that in this respect they appeared to resemble mistletoe. It is hardly surprising that it was believed that tropical orchids were parasites; witness an article in the *Botanical Register* (1815) devoted to *Epidendrum nutans*: 'The culture of tropical parasitic vegetables was long regarded as hopeless with us; it appeared a vain attempt to find substitutes for the various trees each species might affect, within the limits of the hothouse.'

It was only around 1805 that Dr Robert Brown determined the epiphytic character of tropical orchids. Nevertheless, the belief that they were parasites persisted for many years and was to form the subject matter of numerous essays which recommended hopelessly impractical methods of cultivation. This led Joseph Hooker, director of the Kew Botanic Gardens, to remark that for more than half a century England had been the 'grave of tropical orchids'. Certainly the double myth of parasitism and the stifling jungle environment did little to foster orchid cultivation in Britain in the early nineteenth century. Yet despite a variety of barren experiments, the fascination that orchids exerted was sufficient to ensure that imports continued on a massive scale.

all great discoveries, modern orchid culture is not solely due to one man's pioneering work. Many authors, botanists, gardeners, horticulturalists and explorers contributed to progressive improvements. Among various developments which, in gradual stages, ushered in the modern era of orchid cultivation from 1860 onwards, the following were particularly significant:

- discovery of appropriate composts;
- cultivation in hanging baskets (Banks);
- ventilation of greenhouses (Ridley);
- observation of a rest period (Bateman);
- more generous lighting, with suitable shading;
- invention of central heating (Atkinson);
- growing in three different types of greenhouse (Linden and du Buysson).

These innovations made it possible, in the late nineteenth century, to grow epiphytic orchids without major problems. Such rare plants are virtually impossible to reproduce and are thus sold at extremely high prices. They became all the. rage in England, true symbols of affluence. Horticulturalists and wealthy patrons hired collectors to roam the world's remote regions in search of rare orchids. Predictably, matters quickly got out of hand; greed for profit and the desire for exclusive possession led to reckless damage and destruction of the environment. Many species

The nineteenth-century mania for orchids

The Horticultural Society of London was founded in 1809 – it later became the Royal Horticultural Society – significant on many accounts and not least for laying the foundations of systematic research into the various ways of cultivating orchids. Through its exhibitions, too, the Society encouraged passionate public interest in orchids, setting a fashion which eventually took on manic proportions, sweeping the country and enveloping England's continental neighbours by the end of the century.

In this field the man of the moment was undoubtedly John Lindley, who is deservedly recognized today as the father of orchid cultivation. 'Orchids,' wrote Lindley, 'must be grown in conditions as near as possible to those of their natural surroundings.' But like

John Lindley, who founded the *Gardeners' Chronicle* in 1841, made the first definitive classification of orchids in 1830.

vanished forever from their original surroundings: this was the fate of *Angraecum palmiflorum* from the Seychelles, described by Cordemoy, of which no trace remains save in a herbarium of the Natural History Museum of Paris.

In the race to discover new species and stake a claim to exclusive rights on behalf of their employers, collectors ransacked the sites and literally stripped bare vast areas of forest, so that certain species became rarer than ever. This collecting mania, together with the hazards of long-distance transportation and the problems of successful cultivation, conspired to inflate the value of the precious plants beyond all reason. At public sales they fetched ridiculous prices. Lewis Castle, in his book *Orchids* (third edition, 1887), mentions at random the following figures for various orchids sold at Covent Garden between 1850 and 1888:

> 1850, an *Angraecum eburneum*: 19 guineas;
> 1855, an *Aerides schroederae*: £89;
> 1856, a *Vanda batemanii*: £43;
> 1861, a *Saccolabium*: £52;
> 1869, a *Cypripedium stonei*: £38;
> 1883, an *Aerides*: 235 guineas;
> 1885, a *Vanda sanderiana*: £180.

To put these crazy prices into proportion, it is worth remembering that towards the end of the nineteenth century the average monthly salary of a domestic servant was in the region of thirty shillings (£1.50).

So throughout this century there was a ridiculously heavy traffic in orchids. They were despatched to Europe in their hundreds of thousands, carelessly and inappropriately packed, often destroyed by insects en route. Only a small proportion reached their destination in a more or less satisfactory condition. Yet in spite of innumerable failures and losses, the plants could sometimes be induced to flower and thrive in greenhouses.

In 1860 important progress was made when the English horticulturalist Nathaniel Ward invented a closed glass case, virtually a portable greenhouse, in which orchids could be planted in moss or a slightly moist compost. The Wardian case, as it was called, enabled orchids to be transported in far better conditions, although there was still a considerable risk of them rotting.

Noël Bernard and the germination of orchid seeds

Until the end of the nineteenth century germination of orchid seeds remained a puzzle. True, in the mid-1850s John Dominy, head gardener of the famous firm of Veitch, had managed, by trial and error, to get a few orchids to germinate and to raise some hybrids, but there was still no real understanding of how the process worked. Credit for this goes to Noël Bernard, a young French biologist, who one day in 1899 was strolling through the forest of Fontainebleau and happened to notice some young plantlets of *Noettia nidus-avis* around the base of a mother plant. Examining the plantlets through a microscope, he was surprised to find a large number of mycelial filaments enveloping their roots: a fungus that he later identified as a *Rhizoctonia*. Based on this observation, Bernard published a series of remarkable scientific papers in which he described the precise nature and exact role of the orchid–fungus association in the germination of the seed. This led him to the conclusion that orchid seeds, which are almost wholly without nutritive substances, could only germinate alongside this fungus in a close association that he called 'symbiosis'. This permits the seeds to receive from the fungal hyphae all the nutriment they lack, notably the sugars which

The Wardian case, invented by Nathaniel Ward in 1860, enabled tropical orchids to be transported and kept in prime condition.

'normal' seeds have in the storage tissues of their cotyledons.

This discovery had enormous repercussions. In fact, a short while before Bernard's observation, certain biologists had drawn attention to the particular cultures of microorganisms on which *Rhizoctonia* evidently proliferated. It was left to Bernard to sow *Rhizoctonia* cultures in order to achieve germination. In this way he was the first to get orchids to multiply *in vitro*.

This paved the way, after 1908, for horticulturalists to embark on the cultivation of orchids on a commercial scale. As the practice became widespread, the prices of orchids tumbled and many collectors who subsequently lost their stocks during the war abandoned all interest in the plants.

Symbiosis was the keyword, the obligatory procedure, without which no orchids could germinate; or if they did, the result was monstrous deformities. Bernard was nevertheless convinced that germination could be brought about independently if the seed were provided with whatever it received naturally from the fungus. He therefore began a series of experiments in the absence of fungus, increasing the concentrations of sugar in the growing medium. By this means he obtained germinations up to the intermediate stage between protocorm and plantlet. Unfortunately he died in 1911 without having time to perfect these culture media.

The American biologist Dr Louis Knudsen, who had followed this work, obtained the first 'asymbiotic' seedlings from orchid seeds; subsequently Hans Burgeff improved the procedure by considerably modifying the culture medium. Knudsen is widely hailed as the discoverer of the asymbiotic method, whereas Noël Bernard, to the annoyance of his compatriots, is not always given the credit he deserves.

Professor Morel's meristem culture

In 1960 Professor Georges Morel discovered a method of obtaining several thousands of virtually identical specimens from a single mother plant, even of a rare or unusual hybrid species, without recourse to seed. This was the last major revolution in the world of orchid cultivation and paved the way for the flowers to be marketed on a commercial scale throughout the world. Morel, who died in 1973, thus took his place alongside Lindley, Darwin, Bernard and many other great figures in this field.

Morel had a long apprenticeship in the plant histiophysiology department of the Faculty of Science in Paris (1943–8) and with Professor Wetmore at Harvard University

Noël Bernard (1874–1911)

(1948–51), after which he joined the National Institute of Agricultural Research (INRA) at Versailles in 1951 and later became its director. He gradually won renown for his work on the culture of plant tissues, whether normal, tumorous or fungal and parasitic, such as vine mildew, which he succeeded in growing on various cell colonies. He was equally concerned with the morphogenesis of plant tissues, developing media favourable to the growth of the embryonic tissues (meristem) at the tips of the stalks.

Deductions based on chance observations and on modifications of the nutritive media enabled Morel to obtain adult plants from miniscule implants of meristem. But the notion of dividing the growing tips did not immediately occur to him. In the early 1950s Morel was mainly concerned, with the assistance of his pupil Claude Martin, to devise a method to eradicate viral diseases and, particularly, potato virus.

Some years previously, Cormuet and Limasset, researchers at the INRA, had noticed that the tips of the shoots of potatoes infected by potato virus remained unaffected. This was explained by the fact that the viral particles multiplied more slowly than those of the plant cells. Growing undamaged apices successfully rid the infected stock of the virus.

In 1958 Morel tried the same experiment with the apices of virus-affected *Cymbidium* orchids. A few years later, in 1960, Mme Missonnier, one of Morel's assistants, remarked that an accidental division of the tuber-shaped protocorms produced as many plantlets as there were fragments. She brought this to Morel's notice and he demonstrated the phenomenon to Professor Walter Bertsch (d.1984) in Paris. The latter, realizing the practical importance of this discovery, immediately got in touch with his orchid-growing friends Maurice Lecoufle and Michel Vacherot. It was they who embarked on the first programme of vegetative multiplication of orchids by the dissection and cultivation of embryonic tissues (meristem).

Success was so striking that in 1964 the meristem method of reproducing and raising orchids on a commercial scale was publicized for the first time. It is certainly a difficult method that necessitates a good deal of equipment and cannot be undertaken except in a laboratory.

Georges Morel (1916–73)

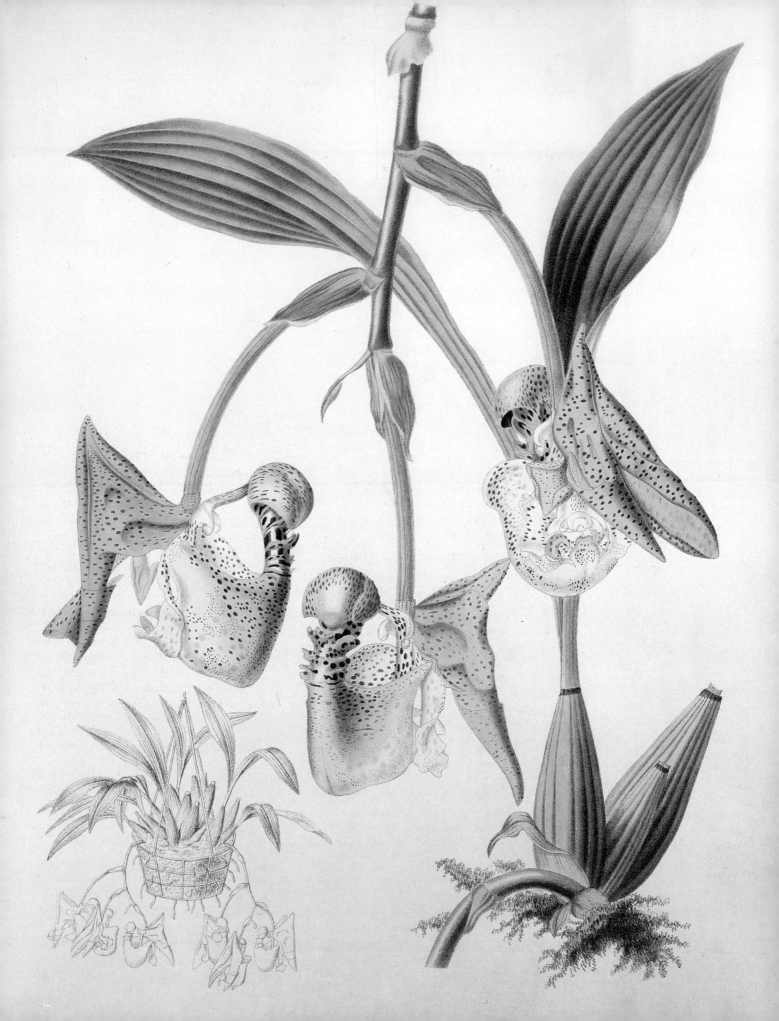

What is an orchid?

Coryanthes originate in Central America and the northern part of South America. Their flowers, of flamboyant appearance and complex structure, constitute insect traps and remain open for only two or three days. (Engraving from the *Pescatorea* collection.)

Despite their apparently innumerable forms and different sizes, and the immense variety of their flowers, orchids make up a family that from the biological viewpoint is remarkably homogeneous. All, for example, have the following features in common:

- enormous quantities of microscopic seeds which are almost or totally lacking in nutritive reserves;
- germination and development made possible by the presence of a fungus with which the plant establishes a close association that is more markedly parasitic than symbiotic;
- the constitution, in the early developmental stages, of a highly characteristic organoid – the protocorm – which subsequently becomes a modified plantule;
- a flower structure consisting of three sepals, three petals – one of them modified into a lip (labellum) – and a single central stamen (except for the Cypripedioideae);
- pollen usually formed into waxy masses known as pollinia; and
- entomophilous pollination carried out by a specific insect for each species; in rare cases (e.g. *Dendrobium sophronites*) the pollinator is a bird or a bat.

Distribution and origin of orchids

Orchids are to be found in every part of the world where some vegetation exists; but their numbers and density vary considerably, particularly in relation to latitude. Thus 3000 species have been recorded in Colombia, 660 in Mexico, 100 in the United States and only 14 in Alaska. In Britain there are some 53 species. Each orchid species has a clearly defined zone of distribution, the area of which may be confined to a few square miles or extend across a number of states or provinces.

In the course of evolution, each orchid has, as it were, made a contract with a specific insect, which guarantees its pollination and thus its reproduction. Written into this contract are the peculiarities of the individual flowers: all the features likely to attract and entice this insect and no other by means of stimuli that are not only visual but also olfactory, nutritive (nectar) and sexual. This explains the insect-shaped appearance of certain species: the entire flower is a 'pseudofemale' lure designed to attract the male who, when his copulatory and disengaging movements are over, will pollinate the flower, carrying away the pollinia to deposit them on another flower. This is a subtle mechanism which, in certain specimens (*Drakae, Ophrys, Coryanthes, Stanhopea* and especially *Catasetum*) is very sophisticated indeed.

This dependence on insects implies that orchids share the same distribution range; and it is natural that orchid genera comprising several hundreds of species should flourish over a far wider area. Study of these zones furnishes extremely important botanical and phylogenetic information. Thus certain genera grow only on a single continent (e.g. *Epidendrum* in America), whereas others, such as *Vanilla* are to be found in tropical regions all round the world. This distribution supports the theory that the genus *Vanilla* is very ancient, a belief reinforced by the fact that these orchids display a number of archaic features. The genus *Vanilla* must, therefore, have been differentiated when the primitive continent of Gondwanaland broke up some 120 million years ago. This deduction, based on the theory of plate tectonics, would therefore trace the origin of the orchid family to the very beginning of the Cretaceous (120–130 million years ago), emerging at the same time as other flowering plants.

Such a conclusion is the more astonishing because in many respects orchids display all the characteristics of a very young family which is still evolving, namely a large number of species which have adapted remarkably to highly varied conditions and which have great potentialities for hybridization. These features, in principle, tend to be reversed in families notable for the age of their species (*Coelacanthe*, *Nautilus*, *Ginkgo biloba*, etc.).

Orchids would appear, then, to form the exception to the rule. Or did they perhaps evolve extremely slowly and only recently reach the peak of their development?

Can all orchids be cultivated?

There are two principal types of orchids: the terrestrials and the epiphytes. The orchids of temperate regions tend to be terrestrial. Like most plants, they develop an extensive root system, with a variously branched rhizome and tuber from which the aerial part of the plant develops in spring and disappears in autumn. Cultivation of this type of orchid is nowadays considered very difficult, given that too little is still known concerning their overall needs, namely the type of soil that suits them and the amount of water and heat they require. For this reason it is almost impossible

to reproduce them. Moreover, a number of these species are disappearing, and it is strictly forbidden to pick or remove them.

Cultivation of orchids is therefore confined to tropical species, many of which are epiphytes and generally less dependent than temperate species on their environment, even though some of them have opted for terrestrial habits. They offer wonderful opportunities for orchid lovers; not only are the majority of orchids tropical but they are far more interesting and varied than the temperate species.

Of the 600 or so genera that make up the tropical flora, about fifty have come under consideration for horticultural purposes; and of these only a handful have been the object of heavy financial investment and intensive research with a view to commercial cultivation and hybridization. These are species of the genera *Cattleya*, *Cymbidium*, *Dendrobium*, *Lycaste*, *Miltonia*, *Odontoglossum*, *Oncidium*, *Paphiopedilum*, *Phalaenopsis* and *Vanda*. Several related genera have been widely hybridized with these principal genera, which are naturally the best known inasmuch as there is abundant information about their generic affinities and the niceties of their cultivation. That explains the emphasis placed on these genera in the present book.

Alongside these highly valued genera are certain others which are occasionally to be seen in botanical gardens. The flowers of these genera are either very small, almost imperceptible, or possess little aesthetic interest, or have never managed to adapt to the cultural conditions prevailing within a greenhouse.

Epiphytic orchids: the principal features

In order to understand the physiology and cultivation of epiphytic orchids, some knowledge of their growth structure is clearly important. The following sections therefore summarize the main characteristics of the different parts of these plants: the roots, the stem, the leaves, the flower, the seeds and their germination.

■ Aerial roots
Apart from the role played in anchorage and nutrition, common to all roots, those of epiphytic orchids also perform the functions

The annual cycle of European orchids. These only appear above ground for a brief period, the aerial parts disappearing towards the end of the summer.

The vast majority of tropical orchids are epiphytes, sometimes with enormously developed root systems. The physiology of these aerial roots determines their different methods of cultivation.

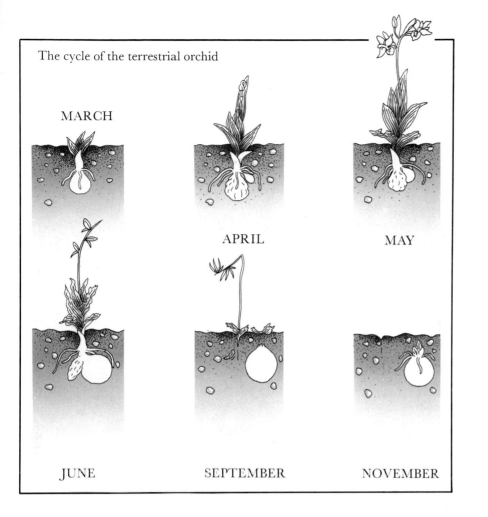

The cycle of the terrestrial orchid

MARCH

APRIL

MAY

JUNE

SEPTEMBER

NOVEMBER

Examples of an epiphytic orchid.

of storage, respiration and even photosynthesis.

In sympodial* orchids, the roots develop from the rhizome; in monopodial** orchids, the roots are thrown out from the stem and are generally at right-angles to the leaf. In their natural environment the roots may be so large compared with the rest of the plant as to constitute some two-thirds of its mass. This is a result of the plants adapting to the extreme conditions in which they live. The more highly developed the roots, the greater the possibilities of gathering the few mineral salts and other nutritive substances dissolved in rain water or morning dew. In the *Grammatophyllum* species, the roots form a dense clump which can retain any plant debris deposited there.

The roots are covered by a vital organ called the velamen. This pearly white, spongy layer is differentiated from the epidermis of the root and covers the whole root apart from the first few millimetres at its tip. The tissue possesses truly remarkable properties; it can absorb large amounts of water very rapidly, like blotting paper, enabling the root to take in water over a considerable period. Once dry, the velamen again assumes it shiny white appearance. It also provides the root with a great deal of protection against cold or dry conditions. When in contact with the bark of a tree, it forms a layer of adherent cells which attach the plant very firmly to its support and often make it difficult to detach.

Roots often have a respiratory function which is sometimes as important as that of the leaves. For this to occur, it is essential that the velamen dries out, at least partially, between waterings. To this end, three cultural precepts must be observed:

● a sufficient interval between waterings;
● correct drainage for the pot, which should not retain too much water; and
● adequate aeration of the roots inside the pot.

*Sympodial growth derives from a lateral shoot and is therefore of horizontal habit (*Bulbophyllum, Coelogyne*).

**Monopodial growth derives from a terminal shoot and is thus of vertical habit (*Vanda, Angraecum*).

Finally, photosynthesis can, to some extent, be effected by the roots, as is evident from the fact that the root tips may take on a green coloration. In certain orchids, this function is assumed by the roots alone: their leaves then atrophy (semi-aphyllous plants, e.g. *Chiloschista usneoïdes*) or even vanish (aphyllous plants, e.g. *Microcoelia*).

The appearance of the roots is obviously one of the most important signs of the plant's health. The pearly white sheen may fade more or less normally with age; but if this occurs too early, it may be an indication of something wrong, for example:

● over-watering;
● incorrect feeding;
● decomposition of compost.

■ Leaves

Most orchids are slow-growing, economical plants which bear only a small number of leaves. These may exhibit a wide range of forms from one genus to another or even within the same genus (e.g. *Dendrobium*): oval or lanceolate, flat or folded, naked or pubescent, deciduous or persistent, thin or succulent, overlapping, cylindrical, paddle-shaped, recurved or upright.

In the majority of genera the leaves have parallel veins, a characteristic that shows that the Orchidaceae are monocotyledons, and probably affiliated with the Liliaceae.

Adaptation to drought and heat is indicated by a thick cuticle and a thickening of the leaf itself, which takes on a succulent appearance and becomes a genuine storage organ. In order to limit, as far as possible, loss of water during the day, the upper part of the blade (lamina) may have no stomata, which are present only in the lower part. Moreover, when it is very hot, these stomata only open at night; the gaseous exchanges without which photosynthesis cannot occur are therefore deferred, which greatly complicates the process (diurnal photosynthesis, nocturnal respiration). In the majority of cases, however, the stomata open widely as the temperature rises, so that consequent evaporation and cooling can counteract an excessive increase of internal temperature.

The cylindrical, channelled leaves of *Vanda teres* constitute a measure of supplementary adaptation to heat and direct sunshine,

giving a minimum amount of heating per unit of surface area.

Finally, in certain species (e.g. *Catasetum*, *Calanthe* and some *Dendrobium* species), the leaves, which are only borne by the new shoots, are deciduous; they turn yellow and then fall in the autumn to leave a bare bulb, which serves as a storage organ for the next shoot.

The structure and appearance of the leaves provide a number of indications for conditions under cultivation:

● the thicker the leaves, the less the plant needs watering;
● if the leaves are deciduous, the plant must have a period of prolonged and absolute rest;
● if the leaves are tender and persistent, the plant must be kept constantly moist, with uninterrupted watering;
● if the leaves are cylindrical, this is a warm house plant which can be exposed to full sun.

Daily examination of the condition of the leaves is of prime importance. Apart from attacks by various pests (insects and snails), daily checks can help to detect or prevent the spread of diseases (e.g. viruses, black rot), avoid the risk of burning as a result of too much sun, and make sure that the plant is getting adequate lighting.

The beauty of orchid leaves can be an additional attraction. This is particularly the case with the superb leaves of *Haemaria* (*Anoectochilus*) which are velvety and reddish with thin golden yellow or white veins. The leaves of some plants (*Lockhartia*, *Maxillaria*, *Brassavola*, *Paphiopedilum*, *Phalaenopsis*, etc.) display a truly sculptural beauty.

■ Stem and pseudobulbs

The general bearing of the plant is determined by the stem. Epiphytic orchids have two kinds of stem, characteristic of two forms of growth: a creeping stem (sympodial growth) or an upright stem (monopodial growth).

The growth of sympodial orchids is derived from a creeping stem or rhizome on which one or several shoots develop from year to year. Each shoot grows into a pseudobulb, bearing one or more leaves, and an inflorescence. The latter may appear either at the top of the pseudobulb (*Cattleya*) or at the base, when it is directly attached to the rhizome

Vanda teres. The cylindrical leaves of this species are adapted to direct exposure to the tropical sun. This adaptation to intense heat tends to restrict greenhouse cultivation of the genus in temperate regions of Europe.

(some *Coelogyne* species) or even on the pseudobulb of the previous year (some *Dendrobium* species).

The pseudobulbs may be packed closely together, almost joining (*Cymbidium*) or some way apart on the rhizome (*Bulbophyllum*) – thus posing some problems when it comes to repotting.

The monopodial orchids have an upright stem with a terminal shoot, from which leaves, inflorescence and aerial roots progressively develop (*Vanda, Angraecum*). This type of growth often gives the orchid a liana-like appearance (*Vanilla*). The record length of 60 ft (18 m) belongs to the genus *Gastrodia*.

In some cases, the stem is non-existent or atrophied, as in *Phalaenopsis* (monopodial orchid) or *Paphiopedilum* (sympodial orchid). Such plants are said to be acaulous.

The two methods of growth have a determinant bearing on their cultivation: monopodials may reach a considerable height, while sympodials have the annoying habit of escaping from their pot.

The pseudobulbs, which may be regarded as branches of limited growth, assume a wide variety of forms. They are cylindrical, fusiform, ovoid, globular or flattened laterally, while some, like those of *Dendrobium*, are long and stick-like with numerous internodes. They are storage organs with the role of retaining water and mineral salts, especially when the plant is confronted with a period of severe drought; when the plants are cultivated, such periods of drought and rest must, of course, be observed.

■ Flower

Although the flowers of orchids are very different, they are all based on an unchanging structure which botanists call the floral diagram. 'The marvellous fantasy that characterizes flowers depends exclusively on the innumerable modulations on this unvarying architecture' (G. Mangenot).

General flower structure

The floral diagram of the Orchidaceae exhibits clear analogies with that of the Liliaceae, suggesting a possible relationship whereby the orchids may represent a line issuing from the order Liliales. Common features with representatives of this order (which include lilies and narcissi) are a pistil formed of three carpels and an inferior ovary situated below the perianth.

Yet important differences distinguish the orchids from the lilies:

- in lilies there is radial symmetry of the perianth (actinomorphism), whereas in the orchids the perianth is bilaterally symmetrical (zygomorphism);
- the six stamens of the Liliales are reduced to only one in the Orchidaceae (except the Cypripedioideae which have two stamens and the Apostasioideae which have three);
- finally, there is a fundamental difference in the formation of the column; in orchids the receptacle extends from the ovary and fuses the single stamen (or the two stamens) and the pistil into a single reproductive organ called the column. At the end of the column are one or two anthers and two or three stigmas linked into a single stigmatic cavity. The third stigma is sterile and is transformed into a rostellum.

Monopodial orchids have a vertical growth habit. The new shoot develops at the top of the stem. The aerial roots appear lower down and attach the plant to its support. These orchids sometimes grow like lianas to a considerable height.

A symisodial orchid: *Cattleya*. This type of orchid develops from a horizontal, creeping stem, the rhizome. Every year one or two shoots form from the lower part of the frontal pseudobulb, producing a new portion of rhizome and a new pseudobulb.

JANUARY

APRIL

AUGUST

NOVEMBER

The different parts of the flower

SEPALS. These are the outermost elements, three in number. During the formation and development of the bud, they play a protective role; their margins touch one another but never overlap. When the bud opens, they take on a petal-like appearance, this being a characteristic shared with the lilies.

Although the sepals almost invariably display a certain degree of bilateral symmetry, the two lateral sepals differ markedly from the central one in shape and sometimes in colour. As a rule they are thicker in texture than the petals.

Certain genera show structural modifications: the sepals may be partially or totally fused to make a single floral part (*Paphiopedilum* or *Restrepia*), or by fusing partially may become the major element of the flower (*Masdevallia*).

PETALS. There are also three petals, the two lateral ones being symmetrical and almost always simple in form, the central one modified into the labellum or lip. They may be vestigial (as in *Masdevallia*). The lip is a very complex and variable flower structure, with the principal function of attracting an insect, transforming itself, as the case may be, into a pseudo-female (*Ophrys*), a flag (*Oncidium*, *Miltonia*), a landing platform marked with stripes (*Zygopetalum*), a trap (*Bulbophyllum*), or a tunnel (*Cattleya*, *Sobralia*, etc.).

The lip is always situated opposite the column. Its purpose is not only to entice the insect but also to guide it, so that it finds itself in exactly the correct position and ready to execute the precise movement which will permit the removal and adherence of the pollinia to a part of its body, and then the attachment and deposition of the pollinia in the stigmatic cavity of another flower. For this purpose the lip is provided with all manner of appendices, superstructures, projections, crests, nectar-bearing spurs, pseudo-stamens, odoriferous glands, false mirrors and the like, the variations being so striking from one genus to another as to defy any attempt at a general description.

The orchids, and their lips in particular, provide a spectacular example of the way in which original structures help to determine plant evolution.

The necessity of being pollinated by the same type of insect has also led to plants from different groups developing identical forms or at least taking on such an apparent family resemblance that botanists have sometimes improperly regrouped them. This explains why many *Oncidium* cannot be hybridized with one another. The puzzle was resolved when their chromosomes were charted: certain *Oncidium* have 56 chromosomes, others 40 to 42. These last figures prove that this subgroup belongs to a neighbouring group or taxon, *Comparettia* (Dressler). This observation lends support to the theory of 'morphogenetic fields' (Sheldrake), according to which the emergence of an efficient form which provides a solution to a problem (in

The floral diagram. Ancestral orchids were differentiated from Liliales, the floral diagram of which shows many similarities to that of the Orchidaceae. Apart from the smaller number of stamens (one in Orchidaceae, except members of Cypripedioideae which have two), the major change is the appearance of bilateral symmetry instead of the radial symmetry of the Liliales.

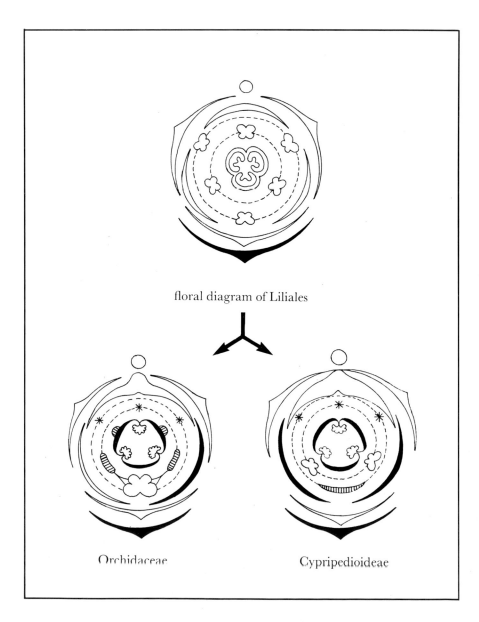

floral diagram of Liliales

Orchidaceae   Cypripedioideae

this case pollination by a particular insect) must make it likely that a similar solution will be found in any part of the world where this same problem happens to occur.

Although this theory still finds scant acceptance among biologists, it could revolutionize ideas about evolution by recognizing the role played by determinism – something that has been strongly disputed for several decades – and admitting that it may provide an answer to the puzzling examples of convergent evolution (the appearance of the same characteristics or forms in plants which are not phylogenetically related). The processes of evolution would thus be seen to be

Below: pollination, often effected by wasps.
1 Attracted by colour, scent or nectar, the insect enters the flower.
2 As the insect prepares to exit, the lower part of its thorax raises the hood of the anther, which protects the pollinia. These stick on to the back of the insect, who thus carries them away.
3 The insect now enters another flower.

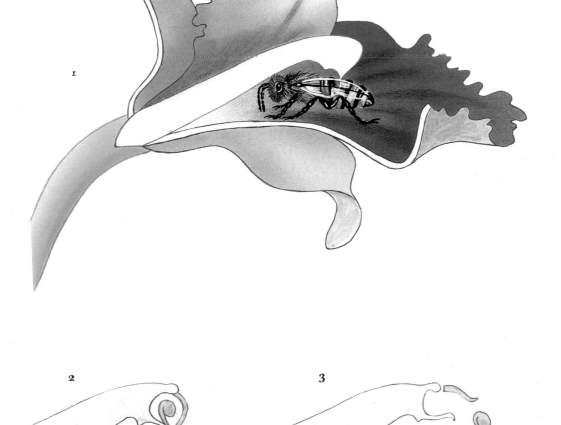

activated, beyond all question, by necessity and not simply by chance.

COLUMN. This central structure contains the male and female reproductive organs, stamens and stigma. On a line with it, beneath the petals and sepals, is the inferior ovary, formed of three carpels. The ovary resembles a flower stalk and is often twisted in a movement known as resupination, whereby the lip of the flower, normally uppermost, as in the bud, is moved to lie underneath the other flower parts.

The column also exhibits a wide variety of details and shapes. At its tip is the anther, formed of the pollen masses or pollinia which may or may not be covered by an easily removable protective hood; the anther is connected by a caudicle to a sticky, projecting pad called the viscidium, which adheres to the body of the pollinating insect.

Just below the anther, and separated from it by a lobe known as the rostellum, which is designed to prevent any possibility of self-pollination, is the stigmatic cavity, shaped like a dome, designed to receive the pollinia from the insect.

The form of the column, the number and consistency of the pollinia and the presence or absence of a viscidium are major taxonomic criteria on which most orchid classifications depend. The column, in fact, is a masterpiece of precision, unique to the plant kingdom, its operation being strictly determined by the structure of the lip which it faces or envelops.

Pollination

Orchids are pollinated by insects which carry the individual grains of pollen, massed inside the pollinia, to another flower. When successful, this is a remarkably economical means of pollination, utilizing virtually all the pollen grains.

The ova do not undergo any modification until the pollen grains begin to develop pollen tubes inside the tissues of the column, reaching out towards the ovary and eventually fertilizing them. The duration of this journey of the pollen tubes and the ripening of the grains varies from 3 to 18 months, a length of time which, according to some authors (cf. the works of Yvonne Veyret) is proportional to the degree of evolutionary development of the genus concerned.

■ The seeds

After a maturation period that may be quite lengthy, the ovary, having now become a capsule or fruit, releases an enormous quantity of microscopic seeds (more than three million in the case of the *Coryanthes* species). These seeds have a very special structure: apart from their tiny size (the widest dimension is only about 0.5 mm), they are extremely lightweight, with a superstructure that fills with air, and thus the slightest breeze will disperse them. Almost wholly lacking any nutritive substance (there is no albumen), the seeds contain an embryo of between 8 and 100 undifferentiated cells (the number varies according to species). Under natural conditions, they are viable for several weeks.

Germination

Only an infinitesimally small number of these seeds find sufficiently favourable conditions in nature for germination and development as a plantlet. Yet, without human intervention,

The embryo contained in the seed develops into a protocorm and then into a young plantule.

seed

protocorm

young plantlet

the plantlet grows

circumstances would appear to ensure that a species can reproduce and flourish in suitable environments. Such circumstances must include the presence of an appropriate fungus which, as mentioned, supplies the embryo with all the necessary nutritive substances; that accomplished, the embryo grows into a cellular mass, the protocorm, measuring about 1 mm long. This organoid, still by nature an embryo, is furnished with rudimentary roots and leaves; but it takes several months for the plantlet formed from the protocorm to be capable naturally of producing sufficient chlorophyll to photosynthesize, which will enable it gradually to become independent of the fungus. This dependence varies greatly from one genus to another, as was shown by Noël Bernard. The more highly evolved the genus, the stronger the link.

Orchid seeds are extremely light and are freely dispersed by the wind.

Classification of orchids

Every system of classification should reflect a natural order, but in the case of orchids the situation is unbelievably complicated. How is it possible, by observing and studying the 25,000 or so species of orchids that exist worldwide, to form any idea as to how they have evolved and become differentiated in the course of time? What criteria can be used to group them in such a way as to take into account their potential genetic affinities? Little wonder that botanists, past and present, have come up against such a wealth of complex problems in their attempts to formulate a coherent classification.

The task of taxonomists (specialists in classification) is all the more difficult because there are extremely few orchid fossils, since for various reasons these plants are highly unsuited to fossil formation. The existence of such fossils would, needless to say, have been invaluable for establishing a so-called natural classification, based on archaic forms that would provide a clue to orchid evolution and an understanding of the genetic affinities of modern forms. Unfortunately, the most ancient orchid fossil dates back no more than twelve million years, all too little in relation to present-day notions as to the origins of this family, but too much in the context of ideas prevailing 10–20 years ago. Orchids, in fact, are plants which are still in an active phase of evolution, as indicated by a multitude of species that are often capable of being hybri-

dized. This might suggest that it is an extremely young family which, in the opinion of some botanists, appeared on Earth only about two million years ago. This, surely, presents a paradox that must lead us to reconsider many of our conceptions relating to the organization of living things.

In fact, orchids are a very ancient and, at the same time, extraordinarily 'evolutive' family. As a result, it is the most diversified of all families of flowering plants.

In simple terms, the task of botanical classification might be compared with that of someone who tried to establish a system embracing all the motor vehicles currently on the roads. Should they be arranged according to marques, type of use or age? Would it make more sense to group a 1918 Ford alongside a Peugeot of the same age, or to put that old Ford together with the latest model (as, by analogy, Dressler has done)? Obviously the choice of criteria is extremely difficult.

After a good deal of trial and error, it now transpires that the most reliable criteria, i.e. those which best reveal the relationship between species and genera, are the structural features of the sexual organs (anthers and pollinia) and hence, in the case of orchids, the structure of the column, the pollinia, the viscidium and the stigma. Linnaeus, in the early eighteenth century, deserves credit for having underlined the merit of this method of classification. More recently, the examination of

Encyclia fragrans. Originally from Mexico, Peru, Ecuador and northern Brazil, many of the species which were long attributed to the genus *Epidendrum* have recently been allotted an independent genus, *Encyclia*.

embryonic forms has emerged as an excellent taxonomic criterion (cf. the works of Yvonne Veyret), in accord with the ideas of other authors who have based their classification on macroscopic criteria. However, one of the most decisive criteria is still the study of chromosomes, particularly their numbers.

Many other criteria may also be utilized as a possible reference for classification, such as the form, function or structure of this or that vegetative or floral organ. But their value is, in most cases, merely complementary. It has often happened, indeed, that the same characteristic will have appeared at different moments in the evolution of different subfamilies or distinct tribes. This seems to be the case in epiphytism but also of numerous other features.

Although, to some, orchid classification may seem a fruitless exercise, the purely intellectual pursuit of grouping plants with common origins and characteristics is in itself rewarding, while for growers the value is immense. Close relationship points to the existence of close inherited genetic traits and thus important possibilities for hybridization. Moreover, although there are many exceptions, close relationship often implies common cultural needs.

Dressler's classification

Among the principal authorities in the classification of orchids over the years are John Lindley (1860), Rudolf Schlechter (1926), Robert Dressler (1974) and Peter Hunt (1978). Although all classifications proposed to this day remain the subject of debate and controversy, the one referred to most frequently is that of Robert Dressler.

His method of classification distinguishes the following categories of groups or subsidiary groups (taxons):

- subfamilies (six for orchids)
- tribes
- subtribes
- genera
- species
- varieties

Much controversy has surrounded this classification (as it has others); and different

Carl von Linné, or Linnaeus (1707–78), founder of modern natural history, introduced the binomial denomination of living things. His methods of classification still apply today.

authors have challenged it on particular points:

- Should one subfamily or part of a subfamily be included in another? Or should two subfamilies be grouped to make a third? Thus Garay's classification takes a part of the Orchidoideae, a part of the Epidendroideae and the Spiranthoideae to make up the single subfamily Nettioideae (see diagram on p. 31).
- Should two or three closely related genera be combined in a single one (as with *Bulbophyllum* and *Cirrhopetalum*, or *Dracula* and *Masdevallia*)?
- Should a variety become a distinct species?
- Should a genus be broken up?

These discussions are often superficial, not to say irritating, because they sometimes give the impression that, in nature, such precise limitations and categories do not exist. But they do have the merit, in many instances, of furthering knowledge of orchids whilst enabling botanists themselves to establish their own rudiments of classification according to their personal preconceived ideas; broadly speaking, they go in for lumping or splitting.

It is now generally believed that the orchids became differentiated about 120 million years ago, deriving from the ancestral order

Liliales. Of these the Cypripedioideae and, above all, the Apostasioideae (very archaic orchids) would seem to be closely related, at least with regard to the structure of the column (two fertile stamens in the Cypripedioideae and three in the Apostasioideae).

According to Dressler, there are four subfamilies of orchids characterized by the presence of one fertile stamen, with pollen

Diagram by Robert L. Dressler. This diagram constructed by Dressler suggests the possible interrelationships of the principal orchid subfamilies and tribes. L. A. Garay proposes markedly different groupings (dotted lines).

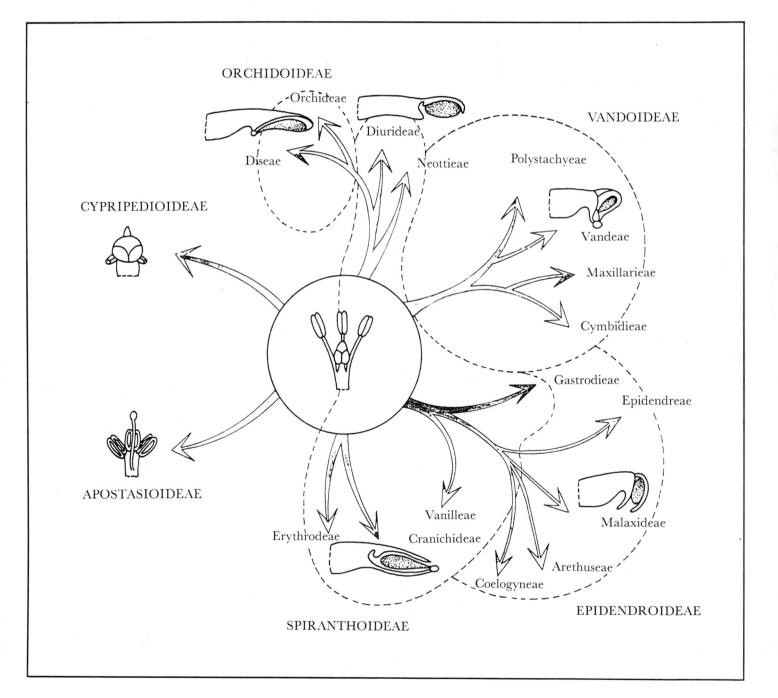

clustered in masses of pollinia; the structure of the pollinia and of the column distinguishes between these subfamilies:

- Orchidoideae: one anther joined to the column, pollinia divided into packets and linked to a viscidium. These plants are almost exclusively terrestrial.
- Spiranthoideae: the stamen is affixed to the rear of the column; the pollinia are soft and friable; the viscidium is anterior. These plants are also almost always terrestrial.
- Epidendroideae: the stamen is protected by an easily lifted operculum; the pollinia are waxy in texture, with an adherent part but no viscidium. These plants are either epiphytic or terrestrial.
- Vandoideae: the stamens are protected by an operculum, the pollinia are attached to one or two hard viscidia. These plants are almost exclusively epiphytes.

By taking into account many other features of both the plant and flower apparatus, the four subfamilies are divided into twenty-one tribes:

- subfamily Spiranthoideae;
- — tribe Erythrodeae
- — tribe Cranichideae
- subfamily Orchidoideae:
- — tribe Neottieae
- — tribe Diurideae
- — tribe Orchideae
- — tribe Diseae
- Anomalous tribes
- — tribe Triphoreae
- — tribe Wullschlaegelieae
- subfamily Epidendroideae:
- — tribe Vanilleae
- — tribe Gastrodieae
- tribe Epipogieae
- — tribe Arethuseae
- — tribe Coelogyneae
- — tribe Malaxideae
- — tribe Cryptarrheneae
- — tribe Calypsoeae
- — tribe Epidendreae
- subfamily Vandoideae:
- — tribe Polystachyeae
- — tribe Vandeae
- — tribe Maxillarieae
- — tribe Cymbidieae

There is no intention in this book of studying in detail the characteristics which led Dressler to establish these tribes, then to divide them into subtribes, which are in turn broken down into more than 750 genera (if one includes the Apostasioideae and Cypripedioideae). For more information on the subject, it is sufficient to refer to Dressler's own work on orchid classification, to which we partly refer.

Another contemporary classification is that of Vermeulen, which divides the order Orchidales into three families: Apostasiaceae, Cypripediaceae and Orchidaceae.

Peter Hunt adopts this system but, instead of Vermeulen's families, uses the term subfamilies.

The naming of orchids

Since Linnaeus and his binomial system of nomenclature, the habit has been to describe living things by two Latin terms, one being the name of the genus, the other of the species. But nomenclature is much more than just giving an organism a label; there has to be a large amount of additional information to the chosen name:

- reference to the common features of all plants of the same genus;
- recognition of a sufficiently large difference between two specimens to justify the attribution of two different specific names;
- position of the named plant within its classification, theories as to its origins and its phylogenetic affinities with plants of the same group.

Nomenclature thus reflects, to a large extent, up-to-date knowledge of the plants in question. This is why the published works of botanists often include changes of name, although these are not accepted by orchid lovers, who tend to be creatures of habit.

The rules of nomenclature are extremely precise, being codified by the International Code of Botanical Nomenclature (ICBN). According to the code, plants are given botanical names designed to define their place within the general classification. The following special endings are used to indicate the particular group or taxon concerned:

Taxon	Ending	Example
Order	– ales	Orchidales
Family	– aceae	Orchidaceae
Subfamily	– oideae	Orchidoideae
Tribe	– eae	Epidendreae
Subtribe	– inae	Coelogyninae

The Latin name of the genus is always written with a capital initial letter and the name of the species with a small initial letters. Both are set in italics. The generic and specific nomenclature is usually followed by the name of the author who first described or observed it (set in roman and often abbreviated), e.g. *Coelogyne mooreana* Rolfe.

When a species originally described in one genus is, after subsequent investigation, transferred to another genus, the first author is mentioned in parentheses, e.g. *Paphiopedilum insigne* (Lindley) Pfitz.

The genus and species may be followed by the name of the variety, e.g. *Chysis bractescens* var. *aurea*.

The nomenclature of horticultural hybrid orchids is likewise subject to complex rules governed by the International Code of Nomenclature for Cultivated Plants. They are described by three names; thus, for example, for the cultivar *Sophrolaeliocattleya* Jewel Box 'Sheherazade', *Sophrolaeliocattleya* is the name of the genus (a combination of the generic name of both parents), Jewel Box is the grex* epithet and 'Sheherazade' is the cultivar** epithet.

Hybridization

When the Horticultural Society of London (now the RHS) was founded in 1809, it soon began to organize flower exhibitions and competitions with prizes and awards that in due course were nationally and internationally recognized. They played an influential role in the growth of the orchid craze which swept England and continental Europe in the latter half of the century. Awards were often based on the strange and novel character of these flowers introduced from overseas; and before hybrids made their appearance, they were given to individual

species. When, in 1856, John Dominy introduced the first horticultural hybrid ever obtained by orchid growers, the *Calanthe* Dominyi, it received the highest award then available. This first hybrid plant, and those which followed, were judged both for their unusual character, which completely upset contemporary attempts at classification, and for the horticultural skill displayed in their cultivation. Their intrinsic qualities were far removed from those recognized today.

Thanks to increasingly successful research into the methods of raising orchids from seed, and following the work of Bernard and Knudsen, crosses became ever more frequent. Uniform tendencies appeared and aesthetic criteria for hybrid (or cultivated) orchids were imposed. Overall forms, mixed and contrasting colours, size of flower, surface proportions of sepals and petals, structure of lip, dimension and shape of tendrils in *Phalaenopsis* species... these are some of the important criteria by which orchids are nowadays judged.

Apart from purely floral standards, growers also concentrate on other aspects: the harmonious distribution of flowers on the stem, mainly with a view to display, handling and transport by specialized florists; prolific flowering; strength of stem, capable of bearing a large number of flowers without support (often a problem with *Cymbidium*); flowering season, etc.

Some growers and orchid lovers talk of 'creating' new hybrids, but this is really a misuse of language. The term 'obtaining' is surely more apt for what is, after all, only a rearrangement of genes, the result of a cross which could not have occurred in nature, given the following insuperable barriers:

- spatial isolation: separate ecological niches for species;
- temporal isolation: species flowering at different times;
- mechanical incompatibilities: e.g. pollinia too large for dimensions of stigma;
- physiological incompatibilities: only those species not too dissimilar will lend them-

---

*The grex is the result of the crossing of two particular related species or hybrids; it may describe a fairly disparate population of specimens.

**The cultivar is a particular individual with precise genetic characteristics.

selves to hybridization. If the relationships (phylogenetic affinities) are weak, fertilization cannot take place or the seed will not attain maturity.

During the 1940s Carl Withner, taking a lead from methods already used for other plants, overcame this barrier in successful experiments involving the aseptic development of immature seeds – this immaturity

From *Calanthe masuca* (lower left) and *Calanthe furcata* (upper left), John Dominy obtained the first horticultural hybrid from two orchids, *Calanthe* Dominyi (*below*).

being compatible *in vitro* with normal embryonic development, even though there was no natural development of the seed within the capsule. He thus made it possible to obtain hybrids from two genera markedly removed from each other (e.g. *Vanda* and *Phalaenopsis*) and opened the way to a new era in orchid cultivation.

At present, important research on orchid genetics is taking place in many countries. The main difficulty is that there is still no way of growing or multiplying a plant cell in isolation from its membrane (protoplast).

Judging panels and awards

For growers of hybrid orchids, awards are equivalent to an official recognition of the qualities of their discoveries, and much importance is therefore attached to them. All the world's major orchid societies give such awards, but because of their age and reputation, two in particular stand out from the rest: the Royal Horticultural Society (RHS) and the American Orchid Society (AOS). Their verdicts are, of course, carefully noted and their shows well attended.

In accordance with established tradition, judging panels sit on average once a month and then make their pronouncements, but the British and American societies each approach the problem differently. The British come to their conclusions more intuitively, without resorting to a points system, whereas the Americans base their decisions more rationally on the arithmetical average of points awarded by the judges. The latter are invited to give a score ranging from 0 to 10, the points representing each of ten characteristics (which obviously vary from one genus to another). So the maximum score is 100 points.

It is interesting to note, nevertheless, that these two methods yield practically identical results. Awards are given the same names, whether from the RHS or the AOS (except for the American HCC and the British PC or Preliminary Commendation). The PC indicates that the judging panel would like to see the orchid in flower again when it is mature and is often given to seedlings in flower for the first time. The points system for the other awards is as follows:

75–79, High Commendation Certificate (HCC)
80–89, Award of Merit (AM)
90–100, First Class Certificate (FCC)

They are subsequently included, in abbreviated form, in the nomenclature of the cultivar, e.g. *Cattleya* Sir Jeremiah Colman 'Blue Moon' HCC/AOS.

These awards are few and far between, so it is all the more remarkable that in October 1985 the French grower, Maurice Lecoufle, took five Awards of Merit with four *Phalaenopsis* and a *Vandaenopsis*.

Additionally, various international, national and regional shows customarily award other prizes in the form of medals. First prize is a Gold Medal (GM), second prize a Silver Medal (SM) and third prize a Bronze Medal (BM). These abbreviations, too, are included in the nomenclature, together with the initials of the exhibition concerned, as, for example, WOC (World Orchid Conference), EOC (European Orchid Congress), followed by the year when awarded.

Orchids as indoor plants

Phalaenopsis Lady Ruby. Provided a few simple precautions are taken, the horticultural varieties of *Phalaenopsis* make excellent house plants.

On the face of it, a house or flat would not seem to be an ideal place for growing orchids. Many of the conditions to be found indoors differ considerably from those that prevail in natural surroundings:

- relative humidity: the air inside a house or flat is, as a rule, much too dry, from 30 to 40 per cent on the hygrometer, far removed from the 70–80 per cent which these plants need;
- lighting: this quickly becomes insufficient the farther the plants are positioned from a window-sill;
- temperature: this would certainly suit most orchids were it not too stable, without marked differences between day and night and from one season to another.

Adjustment of these different parameters to suit the cultivation of orchids constitutes the principal difficulty in the use of orchids as indoor plants. However, various arrangements can be adopted to re-create acceptable microclimatic conditions. Such methods certainly have their limitations, which will be explained in due course, but they offer the orchid lover unexpected opportunities. This is especially true in the case of a window-sill.

Orchids on the window-sill

The ideal situation is a window that faces east, with a central heating radiator underneath. Position a board about 4 in (10 cm) above the radiator, to support one or more flat-bottomed trays which are filled with gravel or pellets of expanded clay, in a layer up to about 3 in (8 cm) thick.

Place the pots on top of the gravel, using an intermediate support to make sure that they do not make direct contact with it, and pour about 1 in (2–3 cm) of water into the bottom of the tray. Check the level of this water every day. A net curtain between the window and the plants will protect them from strong sunshine.

If the window faces south, roller or slatted blinds are indispensable. Since the window cannot be thrown wide open because of possible damage to the plants, the best solution is a window with an upper part which can be opened and closed.

■ Advantages

Such an arrangement guarantees adequate local humidity, which orchids need, but if the whole room can be kept moist, too, with a humidifier, so much the better. In cold weather, warm air currents from the radiator are enough to nullify the possible effects of a ventilator. In summer, movement of air is assured by the occasional opening of the window; even so, it may be helpful to place a small ventilator reasonably close to the plants.

Almost ideal temperatures can be obtained by opening or closing the radiator valve; and of course the heating can be controlled, without personal inconvenience, day and night and according to the season.

■ Disadvantages

This type of system makes it possible to grow only a limited number of plants. Moreover:

- only one category of plant (warm house) can be cultivated by such a method, e.g. *Phalaenopsis*, which thrive under these conditions, or certain *Oncidium* species;
- a west- or south-west-facing window is inadvisable because of belated water evaporation, which may also persist on the leaves or inside the seeds;
- beyond a certain number of plants (assuming the windows are sufficiently wide), the humidity content of the room will rise to an inconvenient level, causing condensation and even mould.

■ General maintenance

Try to observe the following rules:

- water early in the morning;
- provide shade in summer, from 10.00 in the morning to 4.00 or 5.00 in the afternoon;
- check temperature and humidity levels every day with appropriate and correctly positioned instruments;
- regulate the water level in the tray;
- keep a watch on overnight lighting; if this is too strong it may upset the physiology of the plant. This applies in particular to certain species of *Cattleya*.

Orchids on a trolley

This is a highly ingenious construction, used mainly in the United States, which can serve as a model for the DIY enthusiast. But if such

a trolley is home-made, special precautions must be taken with the electrical installation because of the possible dangers due to the presence of metal and water.

The trolley is tubular-framed, 4–5 ft (1.2–1.5 m) high, with three shelves on top of one another. The lighting system above each shelf generally consists of two 40 W fluorescent tubes and one 40 W tungsten tube. Above the tubes is a reflector which bathes the plants in light. At all three levels the plants in their pots are placed on trays filled with gravel and water. The height of each tier

The simplest method of growing orchids indoors. The radiator underneath provides them with beneficial warmth and helps to evaporate the water in the containers.

To facilitate the circulation of air around the plants, it is best to leave some free space between the tray and the wall.

can be regulated and there should be a minimum of 4–6 in (10–15 cm) between the top of the plant and the lights to avoid any risk of burning.

■ Choice of tubes

This applies to all forms of cultivation under artificial light. In theory, it is a question of providing a form of light as close as possible to the solar spectrum. Actually, the physiology of plants, and of orchids in particular, adapts very successfully to a spectrum other than that of the sun, provided that violet and blue (400 nm band) and red (600 nm band) are adequately represented.

Gardening circles suggest different types of

Marketed mainly in the United States, the trolley makes it possible to cultivate up to fifty or so small orchid species, with moderate lighting requirements, under artificial light.

tube, all of which are supposed to give excellent results. Such advice should not always be taken at face value, because successful cultivation obviously depends not only on the quality of light but also on its intensity, its duration and a number of other factors (frequency of watering, use of fertilizers, quality and composition of compost, etc.). Experience shows, however, that all fluorescent tubes will be satisfactory, provided an incandescent tungsten tube is fitted alongside them. This makes up for the lack of red-band light in the fluorescent tubes.

These two types of tube give out a good deal of heat, which is a boon for cultivation provided it is not too strong and that the plants are placed at an appropriate distance. Tubes of 40 W are ideal for the purpose.

It is also worth noting that the heat from the tubes will cause the water in the trays to evaporate and thus increase the surrounding humidity.

Since most epiphytic orchids grow in tropical and subtropical zones, the aim should be to provide them with as much light as they would receive naturally, i.e. 12–14 hours a day. So the tubes must be changed as soon as they show signs of wearing out, in order to avoid too much light reduction.

■ Advantages

This type of orchid cultivation is suitable in conditions where there is little available natural light. Moreover:

- it enables three or four times as many plants to be grown as on a window-sill;
- it is a relatively inexpensive method;
- it is highly suitable for *Paphiopedilum*, certain *Oncidium*, *Miltonia*, *Maxillaria* and a large number of intermediate and warm greenhouse genera that do not need too much lighting.

■ Disadvantages

These are:

- dangers caused by electricity;
- limitation of plant heights;
- rising moisture level in the room, which may be excessive and require ventilation;
- the unwieldy nature of the trolley itself, compensated to some extent by the fact that it is on wheels.

Finally, this system is unsuitable for cool house orchids.

Orchids in a window greenhouse

This quite remarkable system makes it possible to grow fifty or so orchids very inexpensively in a window facing south, south-east or south-west. Ideally it should be accessible from the outside, so that it can be easily cleaned and maintained, and so is only possible in a ground-floor window or on a large balcony.

Naturally, the bigger the window, the better the result. A window about 5 ft (1.5 m) high, with the sill not too far from the ground, is ideal. The greenhouse infrastructure, generally in aluminium, juts out some 18 in (45 cm) from the frontage. The upper part consists of a glass roof, slanting at an angle of 45° or more. In the lower part a basin filled with gravel absorbs excess water from spraying. If too much water collects, an overflow pipe can be fitted. The miniature greenhouse is thus almost entirely outside the wall of the house.

Surprisingly, such a system can create a microclimate suitable for orchids, even if there is no window or other barrier between the greenhouse and the room. This is explained by the fact that currents of air tend to circulate gently inside the structure.

During winter the air is cooler near the roof or top vent, the glass of which should not provide too much insulation. This denser cool air tends to descend, all the more quickly as the walls get cooler. This downward movement is compensated in the upper part of the greenhouse by an inflow of warm air from the room. The drying effects of this are counteracted by the raised moisture level caused by the cooling atmosphere.

During summer the air movements are reversed; air warmed by the side walls rises up and escapes through the roof vent. Cooler air from inside the house finds its way into the lower part of the greenhouse, where it becomes humid before being heated and propelled upward.

These movements of air only occur if shading is provided by an inside screen close to the glass. Any outside shading would cool the greenhouse too uniformly, producing fewer air currents. A black screen is completely unsuitable, because it absorbs too much heat and will rapidly transform the greenhouse into an oven; so a white screen is best.

The window greenhouse is an ingenious way of raising a few dozen medium-sized orchids indoors quite inexpensively.

When it is very cold, the degree of cooling can be limited by 'doubling-glazing' the side and front walls with a sheet of lightweight plastic (polyethylene) which is both transparent and insulating.

■ Results
These are spectacular:

- a perceptible difference of 11–14°F (7–8°C) between the top and bottom of the greenhouse makes it possible to grow a fair number of warm, intermediate or cool house species at three different levels;

- there is constant renewal of air inside the greenhouse;
- the humidity level is quite satisfactory, without affecting the atmosphere of the room;
- the air inside the room is controlled, preventing sudden changes of temperature or excessive heat and humidity.
- the variation of day and night temperatures is much greater inside the greenhouse than inside the room. This fluctuation is essential to the physiology of many species. The minimum temperature of the lower part never falls below 45°F

(7°C), which is perfectly tolerable for the 'cool' species in that area. This assumes, of course, that the house is adequately heated and the outside walls well insulated.

■ Maintenance

This is a matter of observation and common sense, reinforced by readings on the maximum/minimum thermometers and hygrometers which should be placed at every level of the greenhouse. The following rules should be followed:

● the upper roof vent must be closed in winter;

● in spring and autumn, open the upper vent during the day, weather permitting, and close it at night;

● in summer, keep it open all the time (wide or slightly, as the case may be);

● when the weather starts to turn cold, fix a film of polyethylene over the side and front walls; take it off in late spring, when there

is no further need for central heating in the house. This is also the time to spring-clean the whole greenhouse structure;

● as a general rule, watering must be done in the morning. The plants on the upper stages and especially hanging baskets, which are situated in a drier, warmer and better lit area than the rest, will need spraying more frequently.

■ Advantages

These are:

● the possibility of growing some fifty or so plants of all three types (warm, intermediate or cool);

● excellent lighting quality, comparable to that in a normal greenhouse;

● extreme simplicity and low cost (at least compared with an outside greenhouse). This system does not require any complex equipment, nor any heating;

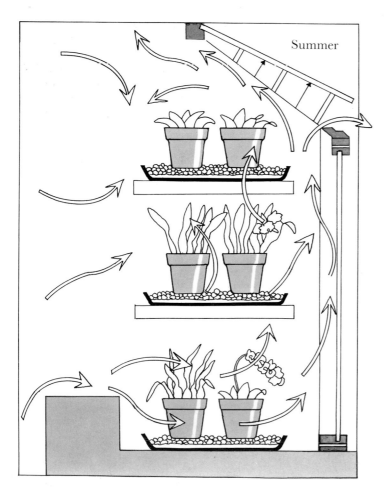

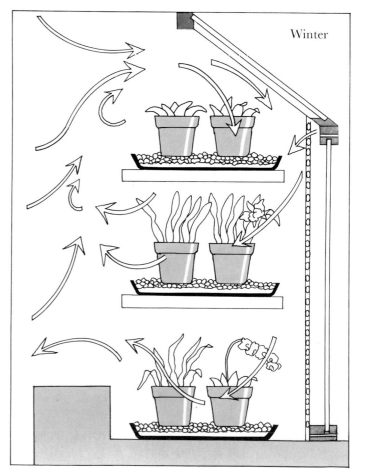

• astonishing results, according to the authors who have tested it (Mary Helleiner in 1980 and Ron Kuhlman in 1983).

The opportunities offered by an ordinary window-sill are considerably increased. It is generally agreed that this type of greenhouse is easy to maintain and that immense pleasure is to be derived from the constant company of one's favourite plants.

■ Disadvantages

This method is not suitable for growing large species. Furthermore, placing plants at three levels above one another means that water can drop down from the plants on top to those underneath, risking the transmission of bacterial and fungal, even viral, diseases from one plant to another. To minimize this risk, some growers place their plants on flat-bottomed trays just as wide as the intersecting shelves, filled with gravel or expanded clay to collect the water and prevent it dripping on to the pots below. But although the trays do not touch one another, the air cannot circulate so freely. Moreover, the visual effect can be very unsightly.

The orchidarium

This is an indoor greenhouse in which all the characteristics of the environment – temperature, ventilation, humidity, etc. – are controlled automatically. Orchid enthusiasts do not appear to be too keen on this method of cultivation and very few publications even mention it. Indeed, the role of the grower is confined to the single task of watering.

Nevertheless, this procedure has its advantages. It looks attractive and the plants are always there to enjoy, especially when they are in flower. On the other hand, they are expensive, uniform climatic conditions restrict their possibilities and, finally, they can only accommodate a relatively small number of plants if a pleasing aesthetic effect is to be achieved.

Other possibilities

There are countless and often highly ingenious alternative ways of growing orchids indoors, too many to mention in detail here. Indeed there seem to be no solutions that have not been thought up by orchid lovers, as is evident from the many articles in the specialist magazines. Apart from window-sills and the above-mentioned window greenhouses, sites include cellars, loggias, terraces, bathrooms, entrance halls, garages, pergolas, attics, roofs.... For those who are determined to grow orchids and who display a bit of ingenuity, it is quite simple... where there's a will, there's a way.

Air movements and heat exchanges help to create a series of local microclimates suitable for the needs of the different plants.

Greenhouse cultivation

Unlike professionals, with a range of green-houses sufficiently spacious for specialization in one or two genera, or even a number of plants with similar requirements, most amateur growers are limited to a single green-house designed to accommodate a variety of genera and species; this can and indeed should provide a range of climatic conditions which make it possible to choose the most suitable position for each individual plant. Nevertheless, a number of species are incom-patible with one another no matter what microclimates are offered. That is why orchids are traditionally grown in three dif-ferent greenhouses: cool, intermediate and warm. It is possible to combine all three types in separate sections under one roof, as was done for the first time around 1870 by the Comte du Buysson. But for this to be suc-cessful a very big greenhouse has to be used, which is often beyond the means of the aver-age orchid grower.

It is essential, therefore, prior to planning the construction of a greenhouse, to decide which option to choose: cool house, interme-diate house or warm house. This will depend on the type of orchid to be cultivated, and also on the local climatic conditions. To install a cool house in a Mediterranean climate would be an expensive matter, as would a warm house in northern England. A cool house, moreover, is not necessarily economical to run; it needs to be heated in winter and some-times in summer as well. Moreover, as a general rule, it is more of a problem to remove heat than to supply it.

Air-conditioning systems have the disad-vantage of supplying large amounts of cold air which are not always evenly distributed over the greenhouse. Cooling systems are more efficient and cheaper, but only practical for the larger greenhouse (see page 46). They have the advantage of solving all the prob-lems associated with growing cool house orchids: ventilation, humidity and tempera-ture. In Britain and northern Europe, how-ever, there is no need to provide such a system for a cool house. The majority of so-called cool orchids will not be harmed by being exposed to heat for several days, provided some care is taken (watering, shading and ventilation) and they are given proper condi-tions for the rest of the year.

Every orchid that lends itself to cultivation may therefore be grown in one of the three standard types of greenhouses. The accom-panying table shows the ideal temperatures, daily and annual variations, and maximum tolerances of each group.

Features of the greenhouse

Many amateurs shy away from the idea of building a large greenhouse because of the heavy cost involved. However, a greenhouse

Wilsonara Ravissement 'Or d'Automne', a splendid trigeneric hybrid of *Oncidium, Odontoglossum* and *Cochlioda*. It can only be cultivated in a cool greenhouse.

SEASON	WINTER		SUMMER	
night/day	night	day	night	day
cool house	10–13°C	16–18°C	10–13°C	16–26°C
intermediate house	13–16°C	18–21°C	16–18°C	21–27°C
warm house	18–20°C	21–24°C	21–24°C	24–30°C

which is too small has a number of disadvantages. Apart from offering limited growing opportunities, it uses up an unacceptable amount of energy. In fact, it is proportionately cheaper to heat a large greenhouse to the correct temperature than a small one. This is easy to understand because if the linear dimensions are doubled, the surface is quadrupled and the volume multiplied by eight. Heat losses (which depend on the surface area) are admittedly four times as great, but the volume is eight times greater. This means that the energy ratio is better, as is the temperature lag of the greenhouse; it is slower to warm up or to cool down.

That is why an ordinary greenhouse should never be too small. The minimum size ought to be 13 ft by 10 ft (4 m by 3 m) and 8 ft (2.5 m) high. Larger structures can have a central bay with plants at different heights and even in hanging baskets. So it is simple to take advantage of the marked temperature differences in various parts of the greenhouse to grow a number of the more important genera. In certain cases, the temperature variation near the roof and floor can be as much as 18°F (10°C). Good ventilation will of course reduce but not remove this difference.

The smaller the greenhouse, the more vulnerable it is to changes in outside temperature. Moreover, and this is important, smaller structures are usually not high enough to grow certain tall specimens properly (e.g. *Odontoglossum bictoniense* or *Vanda*).

Choosing the site

The position of the house and the layout of the garden will usually dictate the siting of the greenhouse. It should not be built in a shaded area, whether such shadow is thrown by the house or by tall trees. Equally, it needs to be sheltered from dominant winds, especially (in the northern hemisphere) those from the

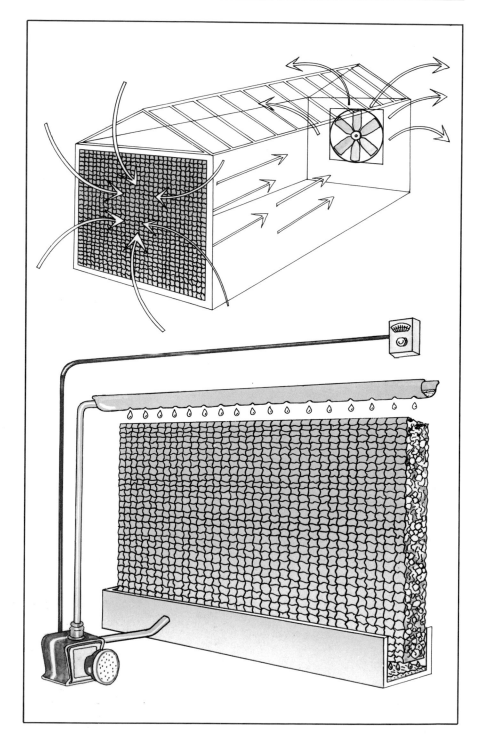

A cooling system cools, humidifies and ventilates the interior of the greenhouse, but is only suitable for a large structure.

north. As an economy measure, it can lean against a wall, although this is not always convenient, unless this option has been chosen deliberately before the building of the house itself, in which case it can be sited in the ideal position, facing south-east. The advantage of lean-to greenhouses, especially if they have direct access to the house itself, is a much easier control of heating and ventilation, plus the pleasure of having the plants near to hand.

A greenhouse is the best method of cultivating orchids. Houses come in a wide range of models which incorporate a number of recent improvements in the quality of materials and superstructures. Moreover, automation has made the growers' work much easier.

Heating

A greenhouse of more than 160 sq ft (15 sq m) can be efficiently heated by electric fan heaters which warm the air while circulating it. Unfortunately, however, these dry the air, so it is worth considering (especially for small greenhouses) an extension to the domestic central heating or an independent hot water system which will provide more regular heat than by convection, with less risk of dry air. The hot water pipes feeding the radiators run beneath the shelving or staging. This solution also makes a separate fan necessary to circulate the air and distribute the heat better.

In very small greenhouses some people use electric oil-filled radiators, with a very low energy yield. But there are considerable risks in installing a high-amperage electrical apparatus in relatively moist surroundings, so this is not recommended. The need for at least two heating systems, one of which is independent of all electrical sources, cannot be too strongly stressed. For the latter purpose a small propane burner linked to the thermostat of the greenhouse is a possibility.

Building materials

Most of the greenhouses now on the market have a light, rustproof aluminium framework which requires little upkeep. They are designed in such a way that the roof vents are of simple hinged construction and easy to operate. Moreover, the panes are fixed in such a manner as to be unaffected by variations of temperature. Heat loss through the metallic framework is limited by the use of battens on the inside surfaces of the frame.

Wood-framed greenhouses are much rarer, but are often more attractive and better insulated. They are, however, more difficult to maintain, for the wood needs treating or re-painting almost every year.

Glass as the standard material for the panes is gradually being replaced by synthetic alternatives which are more resistant to heat loss. Among these plastic substitutes, double skinned polycarbonate has all the necessary qualities:

- excellent transparency to sunlight
- extreme lightness
- excellent insulation

What is not yet known, unfortunately, is how well it can withstand various forms of pollution and, especially, permanent exposure to sunlight. Some concern has been expressed that it may turn yellow and become fragile, as occurs with certain of the older plastics. The initial cost, too, is high. It is essential, in any event, that the inner frame should be absolutely watertight. Condensation of steam can lead to the growth of algae which would restrict the entry of sunlight.

In order to restrict heat loss in the lower section of the greenhouse (under the staging), many builders replace the glass with a low wall of hollow bricks or breeze blocks, the cavities of which are filled with small polystyrene pellets to reinforce their insulation qualities.

The base may be made of concrete with a drainage system for excess water. Alternatively the ground can be left as it is, with paths dug out and covered with gravel. Wet gravel provides plenty of humidity, though sometimes too much.

A couple of water tanks can be set in the base of the greenhouse. One should be used to store water direct from the supply, which can then be treated (e.g. for removal of excess calcium). The treated water can then be decanted into the other tank and stored ready for use.

Openings in the greenhouse

These are the doors, louvred vents, roof vents and box vents (beneath the staging).

The doors can be hinged or sliding. The latter are not very watertight, but are suitable for greenhouses which ajoin the house directly. Doors should be fitted with an adequate closing device which will keep them firmly shut when necessary, to avoid a sharp loss of heat during the winter and thus a sudden change in temperature, harmful to the plants.

Louvred vents should not be positioned so as to expose the plants to direct, strong blasts of air from outside; the angle of opening should be easily controllable. Automatic opening systems are ideal for regulating the greenhouse temperature and enabling masses of warm air to get out, compensated by the influx of fresher air from the outside through the vents.

The roof vents can also be furnished with a simple automatic opening system. However, any openings in the vertical sides at staging level should be avoided as they can stir up harmful air currents.

The box vents in the lower part of the greenhouse will let in cold or fresh air which warms up as it flows over the central heating pipes, so that it does not come into direct contact with the orchids. There can be four to six of these, depending on the size of the greenhouse, and they can be fitted with a device to control their opening. They should be covered with netting fine enough to keep insects out and strong enough to deter rodents, both of which can cause disasters.

Shade: a vital factor

The aim of shading is to prevent the hot rays of the sun penetrating the interior of the greenhouse; for in the absence of shade, the temperature will rise to unbearable levels for the orchids. Dehydration, scorching and loss of flower buds are just a few of the harmful consequences. Whatever solution is envisaged, the shading must always be outside the greenhouse. If, by chance, inside shading has

Cheaper to build than the detached greenhouse, a lean-to greenhouse offers many advantages, including direct access to the interior and the pleasure derived from growing plants so close to the home.

already been fixed, it is essential to double up with another form of shading outside, because although interior shading may protect the plants from direct radiation, and thus from scorch marks, it will do nothing about the rising temperature.

The old-fashioned shutters, made of wooden slats, have now been replaced by lighter-weight shading materials which can be chosen with the rest of the equipment. Shading is, as a rule, 50–60 per cent, according to the region. It is important to choose a material that will be highly wind-resistant and which can easily be replaced when damaged.

In summer, some growers customarily paint the outer surface of the glass, which diffuses the light and thus prevents the greenhouse heating up too much and also protects the plants from direct sunlight. The light thus obtained is better distributed and less intense.

A proprietary shading paint should be used for this purpose. Many professionals use both whitener and exterior shading at the same time, particularly when raising shade-loving plants.

Interior equipment

The staging should be positioned about 20 in (50 cm) away from the central heating pipes. Avoid units filled with compost, sand or soil, or those made of a single section. Repeated waterings will bring about too high a humidity level and, furthermore, the plants will not receive enough air.

Thus there are two possibilities:

- wooden staging with slats $1-1\frac{1}{2}$ in ($2-3\frac{1}{2}$ cm) apart;
- rustproof, large-meshed wire staging.

Wooden staging undoubtedly looks better, but this system does not suit the roots of *Cattleya* and *Phalaenopsis* species, which quickly get caught up with it so that they snap as soon as the pot is moved. Moreover, it has to be scrupulously cleaned and disinfected from time to time with diluted disinfectant.

Wire mesh does not have the same disadvantages. When the roots grow from the bottom of the pot, they simply pass through the mesh. To make sure the surface does not sag under the weight of the plants, it is sensible to have T-shaped metal struts beneath.

In order to improve humidity conditions, it is worth cultivating shade plants beneath the staging.

The big advantage of wire mesh is that it allows better circulation of air and heat. Whichever system is adopted, the space under the staging must never be cluttered up with large objects or shut off by a partition separating it from the gangway, as air must circulate freely by convection.

The ground below the staging can be used, and not merely for ornamental purposes, for positioning plants which need little light, such stay sufficiently wet from the water sprayed on the orchids above, and they also help to control the moisture level of the greenhouse by storing excess water and giving it back through transpiration. Avoid using plants that are too big, which can spill over into the gangway, or with any sharp thorns.

Ventilation

Ideas about greenhouse cultivation have changed a good deal over the years. It is now possible, for example, to modify the environment in various ways, and it is recognized that the quality of plants can be improved by air circulation, either by means of a cooling system or with the aid of interior fans. These methods virtually eliminate any zones of humid or stagnant air which are likely to encourage the development of many plant diseases.

In a small greenhouse it is advisable to install a fan which will distribute the heat evenly. A choice has to be made between a greenhouse which can be heated to a required level but will be restricted in its choice of species, and one which allows for a wider range of temperatures and enables a greater number of species to be grown, bearing in mind that such plants run a higher risk of contracting various ailments, particularly fungal diseases.

Water tanks

Because the water used for watering the plants must always be at greenhouse temperature, some growers find it convenient to install a couple of water tanks for this purpose. One is used for collecting rain water or water from the mains which can then be treated; the other, connected to the first by a siphon, is for actual watering – a small pump with a pressure controller drives the water into the hand lance or sprayer.

Provided they do not impede access or free movement, the tanks can be raised or sunken, made of cement or plastic. They must be designed and positioned so that they are easy to clean and use for dissolving fertilizers, etc. It is a good idea to cover them with a sheet of plastic or some other material to prevent plant debris, soil, dead leaves, faded flowers and, above all, parts of diseased plants falling into the water. Diseases are often spread by recycled water.

Storage and maintenance

Tools, pots, seed pans, composts, fertilizers, fungicides and insecticides should be stored away from the growing area of the greenhouse, in as dry a place as possible. The chemical products, often highly dangerous, must be locked in a ventilated cupboard. Packets, tins, bottles and sachets must be tightly sealed; and it is important to record the date of purchase or latest use with an indelible pen to make sure the products concerned have not gone off and become potentially harmful.

On each visit to the greenhouse it is best to pick off any dead flowers and leaves showing signs of disease, placing them in a suitable container and then getting rid of them immediately. Never leave debris to rot in the greenhouse. Moreover, the container used for refuse should never, under any circumstances, be used for carrying plants or compost, nor should it be put down in any odd spot. It is, in fact, an ideal carrier for all sorts of ailments, and should be disinfected weekly.

Even the smallest greenhouse needs to be kept absolute clean: no plants trodden underfoot, no dried debris, stagnant water, moss or algae, etc., either on the staging or the glass. Sick plants must be isolated so that they do not come into contact with the others; if need be they should be removed or placed temporarily in a corner reserved for this purpose, in order to check or limit the spread of any infection. However, if a specimen shows signs of attack by greenfly, mealy bug or scale insects, it is better not to move it, in order to avoid the trouble spreading, but to treat it on the spot.

Temperature control

It is important to check the temperature in the various sections of the greenhouse and allow it to reach equilibrium before bringing in any plants. This will help you to choose the appropriate position for each plant, taking into account its temperature requirements and height. The temperature close to the glazing must also be checked to find out what conditions the plants have to endure.

In the absence of self-recording appliances, it is possible to use maximum and minimum thermometers, which simultaneously show:

- the actual temperature;
- the minimum temperature (of the preceding period); and
- the maximum temperature (of the preceding day or days).

The staging on which the orchids stand should not prevent the circulation of air. The wooden slats that were formerly used have now been widely replaced by wire mesh, which greatly improves aeration, does not disintegrate so quickly and can be cleaned more easily. Furthermore, it does not provide a hold for roots that often protrude from their container.

These factors allow the plants to be distributed according to their needs.

Humidity, expressed as a percentage of the quantity of water necessary to attain saturation, varies according to temperature. The level is read directly from a hygrometer (which has to be reset from time to time). This is certainly important, though less so if a close watch is kept on the plants' reactions to watering, which is a matter of intuition and experience.

There are alarm systems designed to warn the grower of any threatening dangers, principally those likely to cause extremes of temperature. There are two types of alarm, one to guard against excessively high temperatures, the other against too low temperatures. In the average greenhouse, the alarms will be activated respectively when the temperature reaches the maximum that the most delicate cool house species can stand, and the minimum that the most delicate warm house species can stand, without coming to harm.

Alarm thermostats are placed in the most exposed parts of the greenhouse, alongside the thermometers, and are linked to a sound alarm system in the house itself. Make sure not to turn it off at night for fear of disturbance as this is precisely when an accident may happen. Alarms can also be attached to the telephone, which provides a warning in case of absence. Do not economize in this area, for the welfare of the entire collection may be at stake.

Repotting and composts

The composts in which epiphytic or terrestrial orchids are grown gradually deteriorate, depending on how much water they receive, over a period of 2–4 years. But of course, it is not necessary to wait until decomposition is well advanced before replacing the compost and undertaking the delicate operation of repotting.

If repotting is not done in good time and is tackled too late, the compost becomes packed; under such conditions the roots are not properly aerated, drainage is impeded so that there is too much standing moisture, and the plant will die from asphyxiation and root rot. It goes without saying that certain orchids need repotting more frequently than others, particularly those that have a strong tendency to grow out of the pot.

It is important to remember that repotting always gives a shock to the plant, and the degree to which the plant withstands the effects of such a trauma depends on when, in the course of its vegetative cycle, the operation is carried out. A plant should never be repotted, except in a case of urgency, when it is actively growing or flowering, for this would seriously harm its prospects.

There is, for each genus, an optimal moment in the year for this operation, and there is no specific period applicable to every orchid. Some need repotting in autumn, others in spring. The majority of genera should be repotted every two years, a minority every three or four years (*Cymbidium* and

Restrepia) and a few every year (certain *Calanthe* species).

Containers

It was in the early 1960s that plastic hit the gardening world, transforming all manner of habits and techniques. Even so, unglazed terracotta pots are still widely used. Undeniably more attractive than plastic containers, they also possess a number of advantages. Being porous, they allow some evaporation, and this helps to maintain the root temperature at a slightly lower level than that of the aerial part, which is important when cultivating genera (such as *Disa*) which appreciate such conditions. On the other hand, plants in earthenware pots need watering more often.

Plastic pots have the property of limiting water loss through evaporation and thus the plants do not have to be watered so frequently. This is a great advantage when growing small genera which need compost that is constantly moist (e.g. *Masdevallia*, *Restrepia*, etc.). But plastic carries a greater risk of over-watering and consequent root rot.

The plant is certainly less stable in a lightweight plastic container than in an earthenware pot, but this can be remedied by filling the bottom of the pot with a good layer of coarse gravel, thoroughly washed, a procedure which also improves the drainage.

Big wide-mesh baskets can be used for

Chiloschista usneoïdes. Not all orchids need planting in a pot. Some may be grown on a simple piece of suspended wood. The roots of epiphytic orchids have a multiple function of attachment, absorption, respiration and photosynthesis. When they are well developed, as here, the leaves may atrophy or even disappear.

growing very large orchids (e.g. *Cymbidium* or *Grammatophyllum* species); they can be lined inside with black material pierced with drainage holes.

Hanging baskets of this type are suitable for certain genera, such as *Dracula*, *Acineta* and *Stanhopea*, which have the peculiarity of producing an inflorescence with a downwards habit of growth, so that the flowers snake out low down from among the roots in all directions, drooping as they would naturally from a branch. When such a plant is cultivated, this type of habit makes it necessary to fix three or four large openings at the sides and even at the bottom. A hanging latticework plastic container can also be used, with suitable openings so that the spikes can pass through freely.

Wooden hanging baskets can be used for the cultivation of long-stalked monopodial orchids; certain *Vanda* species will grow in them without any compost.

Repotting

In most cases, if no division is involved, each plant should be repotted in a container slightly bigger than the preceding one. This is not an absolute rule, because the main consideration is to choose a size suitable for the particular plant and its root system. Many people, in fact, tend to use pots that are too large. Once the plant has withstood the shock of repotting, its roots snake out to explore the new surroundings, and the bigger the pot, the longer this takes. Expansion of the roots at this stage entails a corresponding reduction of the aerial part. If the volume of the roots is insufficient in relation to that of the compost, too much water may be retained and this can cause rotting.

■ Preliminaries

Before any work begins, it is important to make sure that the plant is perfectly healthy, absolutely free of aphids, scale insects etc. and signs of cryptogamic or bacterial disease. Treatment with suitable insecticides and bactericides should be carried out a few days beforehand.

On the day of repotting, sort out the plants and tackle them in the following order:

● first, the plants which are completely healthy;

● secondly, the plants which have been treated with an insecticide and/or an anticryptogamic preparation;

● last, and only if you want to take the risk of keeping them, plants with a virus or suspected of carrying one.

Carefully disinfect the work surface, tools and materials, either with methylated spirits or a solution of trisodium phosphate.

■ Tools

The following are indispensable for the repotting operation:

● a stout knife with a strong blade;
● a pair of secateurs;
● a large bucket or dustbin;
● a spirit lamp or small gas heater. The flame of the spirit lamp will be used for sterilizing the knife and secateurs after each plant is repotted and before handling the next one.

The old compost and the scraps cleaned off the plant should be put straight into the dustbin, not left around to dirty the ground and the work surface itself.

■ Preparing the compost

Whether the compost is ready for use or to be made up, it must be brought beforehand to greenhouse temperature and kept slightly damp. Failure to do so is likely to have serious consequences.

On the previous evening, give the compost a good stir to aerate it, so that it can reach the correct temperature overnight. If it is dry, make sure to give it a gentle watering and stir it thoroughly so that it becomes uniformly moist. In the morning, check that the compost is sufficiently damp by placing a hand in the mixture; if no particles stick to the skin, the texture is right. Otherwise it is best to leave repotting until the next day, or even the day after that, stirring up the compost at intervals to aerate it.

■ Removal from the pot

This must be done in such a way as to cause the least trauma to the roots. In most cases (with a small container), it is simply a matter of turning the pot upside down and lightly pressing the sides to release the plant. For bigger plants with roots that are more tightly packed, sticking to the sides or even adhering to other pots, there is no way to avoid break-

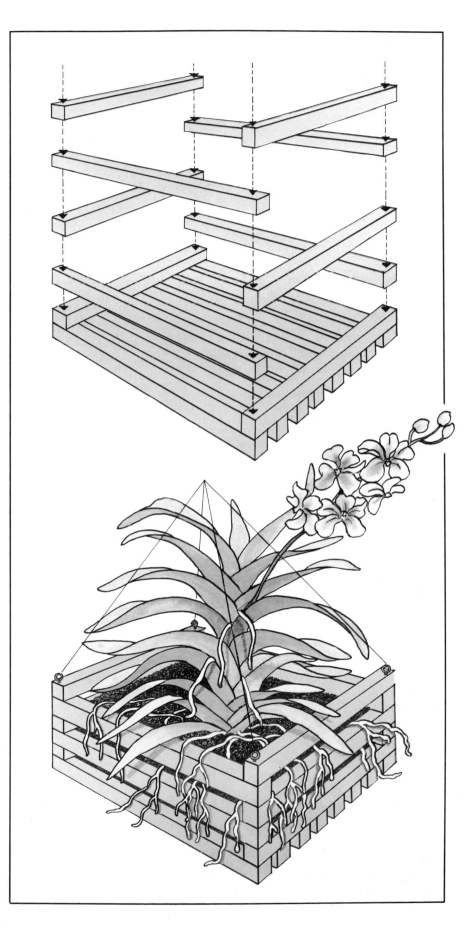

ing them or dividing some of them. If the roots are too firmly attached to the insides, break the pot and carefully remove each fragment. If the pot is plastic, cut it up.

Remove the old compost by shaking the rootball over the dustbin and removing the stickiest bits by hand.

■ Trimming

This is simply a cleaning operation, in which the tools, sterilized in the flame and then cooled, are used to cut away all the dead roots. The live roots situated outside the pot are either cut back (*Cattleya* and sympodial orchids) or retained (*Vanda* and monopodial orchids). The live roots located inside the container are, of course, preserved.

Cut off any dry inflorescences and dead leaves, remove any diseased parts and cauterize or paint wounds with a specific product for that plant or dust them with ground charcoal. If you decide to repot large and rather hard roots (*Vanda*, *Phalaenopsis*), soften them up by plunging them for a few minutes in water at 86°F (30°C).

This is the stage at which the plant can be divided.

■ Centring and positioning the plant

Positioning the plant in its new container is not much of a problem for monopodial orchids such as *Vanda*, *Phalaenopsis* and *Angraecum*, which are placed dead centre. A sympodial orchid should be positioned off-centre in such a manner that its future shoot can develop towards the centre of the pot and its new roots probe down into the compost. In practice, the shape of the plant often leads to unsatisfactory solutions, as, for example, when the new shoot is placed right in the centre and thus needs a pot which is too big for it. Whatever happens, the horizontal growth habit of sympodial orchids necessitates a certain amount of free space in front of the bulb to avoid the plant escaping too rapidly from the pot.

Suspended open-work baskets are useful for cultivating many large epiphytic orchids. They guarantee excellent aeration and drainage.

Repotting a *Cattleya*.

1 Remove the *Cattleya* from the pot if the roots are not stuck to the sides; if necessary they can be detached by gently pulling the pseudobulbs.

2 Divide the clump by cutting the rhizome with secateurs, previously sterilized in a flame.

3 Two clumps are thereby obtained.

Before positioning the plant, line the new container with coarse, pre-washed gravel or with pieces of expanded polystyrene to facilitate drainage, and cover them with a little compost. You can then hold the plant firmly while setting it in the compost.

The rhizome of sympodial orchids should be lightly buried during repotting. It will soon regain its correct position on the surface of the compost as this compacts as a result of successive waterings.

At one time it was customary to use a wooden potting stick to pack down the compost. Nowadays this tends to be done by hand, which causes less shock to the roots and makes it possible, with a little care, to get a smooth and more even finish.

Repotting a *Cattleya* (continued)

4 Throw away the old compost. Roots that are too long are partially cut back and dead roots removed.

5 Place a few pieces of polystyrene or some large pebbles in the bottom of the pot.

■ Staking

There are several types of support, made of metal, wood, bamboo or plastic. Although they do not look very attractive, they are nevertheless essential, particularly for monopodial orchids which cannot find an equivalent of their natural supports (tree trunks or branches) in the greenhouse, and for flower spikes which tend to curve inward (*Cymbidium*, *Phalaenopsis* and *Odontoglossum*).

The stake must be correctly placed, according to the genus:

- for monopodial orchids it should be positioned along the length of the stem, inserted to the base of the pot, the top reaching to just beneath the terminal shoot;
- for sympodial orchids the main consideration is to position it so that it does not impede the development of a new shoot. So *Cattleya* will be supported by one or more stakes placed just behind each branch of the rhizome.

Repotting a *Cattleya* (continued)

7 Fill the pot with new compost so that it lightly covers the rhizome, and firm it down by hand.

6 Position the plant off-centre so that the front bulb has plenty of space.

Ties should not be fixed too tightly, otherwise there is a risk of strangling the plant as it grows. They must support the plant but not crush it. The best ties are of soft plastic, reinforced by metal strips. Twine and wire should never be used because they exercise too much pressure.

■ Labelling

If only to avoid any risk of confusion, each plant in a collection should be systematically labelled with its name and index number. The label is best attached to the pot or plant. Any that are simply stuck into the compost are liable to be lost or, worse still, misplaced.

Information on the label should for preference be written with a medium hard pencil. All other types of marking, with a biro, felt pen or ink, fail to withstand the combined effects of light, watering and feeding, whereas pencil remains perfectly visible even after 20 or 30 years.

Staking helps the plant to grow and to flower in the best possible conditions.

■ After repotting

In the days following repotting, scar tissue has to form over the many wounds sustained by the plant in the course of the operation, whether during the initial trimming, from breaks caused by folds, from cutting of the rhizome, etc. Good quality scar formation can only come about if the roots and the rhizome are kept in a relatively dry condition for about three weeks; if not, there will be a high risk of bacterial or fungal secondary infection. To achieve this state of dryness, it is necessary to stop watering. But to ensure that the plant does not suffer from this deprivation, its vegetal activity must be reduced to a minimum; placing it in shade limits water-loss through evaporation. This evaporation, which could harm the plant, is in any event restricted by the high humidity content of the greenhouse and by the previous dampening of the compost.

In the days following repotting, if the surface of the compost begins to dry out, sprinkle a little fresh water in the mornings so as to keep it sufficiently moist. During the second and third weeks gradually increase the quantity and frequency of water given. After about a month, when the new roots have appeared, resume the normal rhythm of watering. As soon as the roots are settled in the compost, begin applying fertilizer again, as recommended.

These modified operations are mentioned as general examples. In fact, they will vary considerably from one genus to another. Certain orchids suffer very quickly from lack of water; so this should be borne in mind to arrive at a compromise solution. The important thing to remember is that during this entire period a sudden dose of water may be far more risky to the plant than a temporary drying out.

Urgent repotting

An emergency may arise because of various accidents: breakage of a plant, partial rotting, bacterial or fungal disease, application of toxic substances, necrosis of the roots through over-watering or excess salinity, etc. In such a situation, you should:

● remove the inflorescence, at any cost – the plant needs all its active energy to combat the attack;

- proceed as for normal repotting;
- get rid of all roots and dead leaves;
- place the plant, after repotting, in semi-shade and leave it there for three or four weeks so as to avoid all unnecessary transpiration;
- water the surface of the compost sparingly in the early stages;
- resume normal watering prudently after a month.

If all the roots are dead (as may happen in the case of excess salinity), various procedures are possible depending on the size of the plant:

- For a large plant: after normal repotting, the plant should be firmly supported at the compost surface with one or more stakes. Do not water normally, just a sprinkling until the roots reappear.
- For an average plant: either adopt the preceding solution or place the plant in a fairly big pot filled with live sphagnum moss, or failing this, charcoal; both have remarkable antiseptic properties. Sprinkle very sparingly indeed. Put the plant in a warm, humid greenhouse. When the new roots begin to sprout, repot as normally.
- For a small plant: proceed as above or place the pseudobulbs in a plastic bag containing a little fresh sphagnum moss, then inflate the bag, seal it carefully and continue treatment as for the pseudobulbs of *Cymbidium* (see p.129–30).

Compost ingredients

The first attempts to acclimatize tropical orchids in Europe led to experiments with all kinds of substrates. After some unsuccessful trials at the beginning of the nineteenth century, when orchids were simply potted in fresh soil, it was gradually realized that mixtures had to be used which conformed better to the physiology of the plant roots, thus paving the way for modern cultivation.

Some of these growing media are still utilized today, particularly the substrate boldly recommended by Lindley around 1880 for cultivating *Vanda* species, composed of fragments of terracotta and pieces of charcoal. This compost, one of the best possible for such plants (provided they are well fertilized), has

recently caused the death of orchids repotted in it. This happened because the charcoal had been treated to render it more inflammable for barbecues and the roots reacted to the chemical used. So great care still has to be exercised in choosing and purchasing ingredients.

The composts which have been selected progressively by orchid growers, used either alone or in association with one another, should possess the following characteristics:

- the interstices must be left free for the air to circulate so that the respiratory function of the roots is not impeded at any stage;
- water should be able to flow freely, and enough retained for storing and distributing the necessary amount of humidity, without risk of the compost becoming waterlogged at any time;
- it should withstand decomposition for as long as possible;
- it must offer the roots good opportunities for adherence;
- it should promote ionic exchange between the water and the roots;

Acidity of the compost

The various biochemical reactions associated with the activities of the roots, of micro-organisms and gradual decomposition of the substrate cause the latter to become increasingly acidic. The more pronounced this is, the quicker the compost deteriorates. So it is important to be able to control this process, to diagnose it and to prevent it by means of appropriate treatment, particularly in the case of orchid species which only need repotting at lengthy intervals.

The acidity of the compost may be measured by soaking small but equal amounts of the mixture, taken from different spots, in water for at least twelve hours. Measurement may be carried out after filtration of the solution either with a pH-meter or with indicator paper, although the latter is rather imprecise.

A pH of under 5.5 may be a clear sign of decomposition, requiring a repotting. Should decomposition not be the cause of a low pH sprinkle the pot with a small quantity of dolomite lime (coarse powder of magnesium and calcium), which possesses the property of releasing very slowly the carbonates that raise the pH of the compost. Dolomite lime is often added as a supplement to composts when being prepared.

Pieces of marble (of similar chemical composition) play the same role as dolomite. Some growers add it to their compost for cultivating *Paphiopedilum* species.

- it must deter the development of microbes and fungi.

Obviously, no single ingredient of the substrate can meet all these criteria; that is why, over the years, composts with different formulae have been selected, in an attempt to reach the best possible compromise. Inevitably there is argument among individual authors and schools of thought over this or that formula; and it is no easy matter to evaluate the various products, taking into account other cultural imperatives such as light, temperature, rhythm of watering, fertilization, respect for rest periods, treatment with insecticides, etc.

The modern tendency is to conclude that the composition of the compost, although important, is not the sole determining factor in the successful cultivation of orchids. Success depends much more on a sensibly balanced combination of all these factors.

■ Sphagnum moss

This is a live moss that grows in wet places. Long used on its own, it gives remarkable results and holds water well. When growing, it has undeniable antiseptic and vitalizing properties which can be put to profit when trouble arises.

Unfortunately, sphagnum moss goes off quite quickly, especially in contact with fertilizers, and necessitates repotting every couple of years. Moreover, it is increasingly difficult to find and rather expensive.

■ Osmunda fibre

This traditional constituent, the roots of a fern, has very good aeration properties and breaks up less rapidly than sphagnum (three years).

■ Tree fern

This excellent ingredient is highly resistant to decomposition. It permits good aeration of the roots and possesses rare supportive qualities. Tree fern is thus used either in shredded form as part of the compost or as rafts on which virtually all epiphytic species can be grown (as hanging plants). Some adapt to it better than others; it is an ideal form of culture for equitant *Oncidium* or for certain *Dendrobium*, but far less suitable for bigger species such as the *Cattleya*.

■ Oak bark or tan

The custom of using bark has become increasingly common as a means of offering epiphytic orchids a quality of support comparable to the bark of the tall trees on which they grow naturally. Oak bark gives good results.

■ Cork bark

This bark also yields excellent results; it can be used for cultivating many species on hanging rafts. But it may break up under attack by insects.

■ Conifer bark

The major advantage of the various conifer barks is that they resist decomposition much better than cork bark and provide an equal amount of support. Pine and fir bark, especially when used as the predominant ingredient of the compost, may need to be supplemented with a nitrogen-rich fertilizer (e.g. a 30-10-10 formula). In fact, the conifer barks harbour, between their layers, colonies of micro-organisms which are major consumers of nitrogen, a deficiency of which is harmful to orchids.

■ Peat

An organic compound made up of decomposed and fermented sphagnum, peat retains moisture very effectively. Unfortunately it also makes the compost rather heavy and restricts air circulation, so it is not much used, although it is still suitable for orchids with intermediate habits, somewhere between terrestrials and epiphytes (e.g. *Lycaste* and *Pleione*).

Furthermore, peat tends to accumulate and retain salts, which may expose the plants to damage caused by excess salinity. Consequently, it is advisable to rinse the compost before carrying out any fertilizer use (a general rule of feeding).

■ Polyurethane moss

A fairly new ingredient, this moss is quite resistant to decomposition, retains water well and only releases it slowly to the exterior, so it helps to ensure an adequate moisture content within the compost.

■ Charcoal

Provided it has not been treated for burning in barbecues, charcoal is an excellent ingredient, even though it does not hold much water. It has antiseptic properties associated with its power to absorb bacteria and micro-organisms. In powdered form it can be sprinkled on wounds and lesions of the roots, especially prior to repotting.

■ Expanded polystyrene

This neutral constituent does not retain water and thus assists drainage, helping to lighten the weight of the compost.

■ Expanded clay

This excellent ingredient consists of pellets of baked clay, with innumerable microscopic vacuoles that fill with water after plant watering and retain it for a long time. It does not break up or, at any rate, only very slowly. It encourages drainage and makes good contact with the roots, but has the disadvantage of being rather costly.

Raft cultivation

This method of cultivation, which can be in hanging form, comes near to creating natural conditions for tropical epiphytic orchids. It enables many 'difficult' orchids (the needs of which when being repotted are not easy to master) to be grown successfully.

The plants are gently laid on the chosen support (cork, tree fern or log), then, in order to improve the initial development of the roots by supplying extra moisture, a little sphagnum moss may be placed between them and the support. The whole structure can be kept together by a tie, preferably of plastic; or the tree fern raft may be pierced so that the tie can pass through inconspicuously, without spoiling the appearance of the plant.

A watch must be kept, as the orchid grows, on the tension of the ties, so that it continues to be well supported but not crushed vice-like. Orchids grown on rafts and, more especially, on logs and bark have the great inconvenience of requiring very frequent watering; but there is virtually no danger of over-watering.

It has to be said that this growing method adds much to the beauty of a collection and enables a large number of small compatible species to be positioned side by side.

Cultivation notes

Every orchid collection, even the smallest, ought to be catalogued in a book or card index system, so that information as to the origins and cultivation problems of particular plants are always ready to hand. Each plant should be labelled with its name and reference number.

Two types of notes need to be kept:

1 Notes relating to acquisitions:
● date of purchase;
● complete identity: names of genera, species and author;
● in the case of a hybrid: genus, grex, cultivar, awards, parents;
● conditions on purchase: name and address of previous grower, quality of plant on arrival;
● description: number of pseudobulbs, state of leaves, roots and compost;
● any quarantining necessary.

2 Notes relating to habit of plant and details of culture:
● dates of fertilizer application: formula and origins of the product, concentration used;
● dates and nature of pesticide treatments: names of commercial preparations, doses applied;

● accidents in the course of cultivation;
● dates of repotting: nature and composition of compost used, origin of ingredients;
● date of flowering, duration, characteristics.

This list is obviously neither exhaustive nor limitative. It should not be a troublesome duty, rather regarded as a kind of log book to be kept up to date, and certainly indispensable to the long-term maintenance of the collection, designed to prevent blunders and bring to light possible errors.

It is also important to note down:

● hybridizations: label with serial number, cross-referenced to an index card bearing the names of the parents;
● products: fertilizers or pesticides; dates of purchase and use should be entered in indelible ink on the container because many of these products, as they deteriorate, risk causing damage to the plant.

Cultivating orchids on hanging rafts entails frequent watering. Various supports can be used such as tree fern and cork-oak bark or simple logs. Many epiphytic orchids grow best in these conditions.

Light

Light is the indispensable source of energy for all plants that contain chlorophyll. In various ways, according to the species, it plays a key role in the metabolism of carbon and thus in the very construction of vegetable tissue. For orchids, and for other families of plants, the presence or sudden absence of light has a visible effect on the flowering cycle, and this is exploited by growers who, for example, place certain *Cattleya* species in deep shade for several weeks during the autumn so as to retard flowering, with a view to meeting the demands of the Christmas season. In contrast, nocturnal lighting, even if weak, can inhibit or even prevent flowering. This strange phenomenon has so far been noted only in the case of the Laeliinae subtribe, of which *Cattleya* is a genus.

When growing orchids indoors, and wherever they are cultivated under artificial light, the following points must be borne in mind:

- The various wavelengths of light in the solar spectrum have different effects on the plants: blue light, for instance, even in small amounts, plays a determining role in morphogenesis (structural development); red light, strongly absorbed, is all-important for photosynthesis; green is hardly absorbed at all (hence the colour of plants); and too much infra-red can be harmful to certain epiphytic orchids, heating and scorching the leaves.
- The reactions of the different genera and species to the quantity of light received depends on where they originate: the

Vanda species, with tough, cylindrical leaves, are perfectly adapted to direct sunlight and heat, whereas the *Paphiopedilum* species are better suited to the filtered light of the undergrowth. So there is no question of growing these two genera under the same conditions.

- Lighting that does not comply with a plant's needs is a major limiting factor which slows or even arrests its growth entirely, not to mention subsequent changes in appearance or development of lesions.
- Lighting which is too strong but does not provide heat may in the short term cause the surface of the leaves to turn red. This coloration is associated with the presence of photocyanic pigments and is a sure sign of over-exposure. It is more than likely to be accompanied by other disorders, including arrest of growth. A lack of nitrogen and potassium in relation to phosphorus will provoke the same symptom.
- Lighting that is both too strong and too hot will cause leaf scorch, followed, to a lesser or greater extent, by necrosis. There are two ways of preventing this serious trouble: one is to give the plant plenty of shade and air at the beginning of summer, from 10.00 in the morning until 4.00 or 6.00 in the evening; the other is to install (size of greenhouse permitting) a cooling device whereby fresh, moist air can be introduced, so that the plants exposed to the sun may not need to be shaded. This is particularly suitable for many orchids that

come originally from high mountain zones (such as *Cymbidium*), which are accustomed to cold and very high intensity of light.

Modifications of leaf colour provide useful signs of the plant's lighting requirements. A rather pale, predominantly yellow, tone, as well as red pigmentation, are signs of over-exposure; a very dark green colour, due to an increase of chlorophyllous pigments, shows that the plant is distressed and is reacting to the effects of lighting that is too weak by increasing its chances of collecting the few photons available.

Saccolabium atrorubens. Light is an essential factor for cultivating all plants and it must be applied carefully to orchids, since each genus has different requirements.

Water and humidity

Watering is one of the most delicate and important operations in the cultivation of orchids and the maintenance of their health. Epiphytic orchids have aerial roots which have to be allowed to dry out almost completely between successive applications. This goes quite against every natural instinct of the beginner, who tends to believe that the more he waters his plants, the more he demonstrates his love for them.

Adapted to tropical climatic conditions, where periods of drought alternate with showers of varying duration, and where for weeks on end the only water comes from the morning dew, epiphytic orchids are furnished with a surface organ, the velamen, which has the function of storing the maximum amount of water in the shortest time, so that this can subsequently be absorbed by the root. It also facilitates an interplay of ionic exchange between the root and the salts dissolved in very small quantities in this outside water.

The velamen has something like the structure and fragility of blotting paper. If it remains soaked with water (and with mineral or organic salts) for too long, it undergoes bacterial fermentation and is eventually destroyed.

The roots, in addition to their other functions, play a basic respiratory role. If their surface is covered by a film of water, which is a very poor conductor of oxygen and carbon dioxide, there will be no further gaseous exchanges and the roots and the plant itself will suffocate. Finally, it must never be forgotten that epiphytic orchids can better withstand temporary drought than excessive watering.

Given a happy medium between overwatering, which soaks the roots and causes suffocation and rotting, and absolute drought, the compost will retain a slight humidity for hours, or even days, after watering, and this is very beneficial for the physiology of the roots. This is due mainly to the nature of the ingredients in the compost, some of which are capable of retaining water and releasing it very gradually. The time this takes depends on the constituents, but also on the temperature, the humidity level of the greenhouse or room, the size of the container, its inner aeration, etc. In certain cases, after repotting, for example, during the period of complete or partial rest, or when it is very hot, this slight humidity may be maintained by sprinkling just the surface of the compost and perhaps the leaves with a fine-rose watering-can, making sure that no water collects inside the leaf sheaths or around the terminal shoot (e.g. *Phalaenopsis*).

Apart from its physiological role as a vehicle for mineral salts and nutritive substances, water has a complex effect on the metabolism of epiphytic orchids: partly released by transpiration, partly stored for a shorter or longer time in the reserve organs, it

Maxillaria variabilis. This species originally came from Central America and, like all epiphytic orchids, must be watered with care, at intervals which allow the roots to dry out partially between each session.

is also responsible for the elasticity of the plant tissues.

Depending on its climatic and geographical origins, each genus of orchid, indeed each species, has its individual requirements in respect of weekly rhythms and annual cycles of watering, and unless such needs are scrupulously observed the plant will soon be in jeopardy. These rhythms and cycles are dealt with in the sections devoted to specific genera.

Characteristics of water used for orchids

Taking into account the conditions encountered by orchids in their natural surroundings, it was for some time considered essential, when cultivating them, to use only rain water. Unfortunately, the heavy atmospheric pollution to be found nowadays in industrialized countries has to some extent ruled out this cultivation procedure. Nevertheless, it is possible to use it provided this is not rain which has fallen in the last quarter of an hour, having, as it were, 'washed' the air. Such rain, in fact, is often full of impurities: acid fumes, fumes from domestic and car fuels and dust of various origins.

There are obviously practical difficulties involved when it rains while the greenhouse owner is away. One solution is to install suitable pipes, with valves, designed to collect any rain from the roof of the greenhouse or main dwelling and conduct it to the tank reserved for watering.

Problems of pollution apart, it is not always possible to use rain water on its own, either for obvious practical reasons (indoor cultivation) or because there is not sufficient water available to satisfy the needs of a large collection.

■ Tap water
Should there not be enough rain water, the only solution is to use tap water from the mains, but certain precautions must be taken. Although it is useful to know its overall mineral content, this is really a secondary consideration. In fact, it is not so much the presence or quality of this or that element as the excessive quantity of one or the other which may render such water unsuitable for use.

An excess of any of the three following elements is undesirable:

- Excess sodium. This may apply in the case of slightly brackish water supplied in certain regions or countries, which has been 'treated' by softening, and it must be avoided altogether.
- Excess chlorine. This is not really a danger because any tap water to be used for watering will be kept in the tank in the greenhouse for some hours or days before being used, so that almost all the chlorine will have been eliminated simply by diffusion or evaporation.

Coelogyne sulphurea. Originally from Indonesia (Java and Sumatra), this has recently been reclassified in the genus *Chelinostele.*

- Excess calcium. In certain areas (especially those with limestone terrain), calcium may reach a very high level. Although calcium is certainly one of the most important elements for plant physiology in general, and orchids in particular, too much of it proves toxic.

Furthermore, calcium salts form insoluble precipitates, causing micro-crystallizations on leaves and roots. Such unsightly deposits, by their very thickness, can constitute a physical barrier to the photosynthetic process. Inside pots, these micro-crystallizations may represent a serious threat to cultivation.

Epidendrum falcatum. A species originating in Central America: Mexico, Guatemala, Honduras, Costa Rica and Panama.

In most instances, however, the hardness of tap water is compatible with the needs of the orchids, and many growers use it without treatment, except for the addition of fertilizer. A number of terrestrial species, including the *Paphiopedilum*, are in fact calcicoles so they do very well on untreated tap water, whereas epiphytic orchids, accustomed to slightly acid rain, may suffer from water that is too hard, often equivalent to a fairly high pH factor (7.2–7.5).

■ **Water treated with nitric acid**
It is possible to reduce the calcium carbonate content of water by adding a little nitric acid.

The water should be checked (with a pH-meter or indicator paper) until a pH of 6.0 ± 0.1 is obtained.

Very dangerous and highly corrosive, nitric acid must be handled with the utmost care. It is imperative to wear gloves and protective spectacles, and to add the acid to the water, not the reverse, to avoid splashing. The resultant solution of calcium nitrate is easily assimilated by the plant, but is quite insufficient to fulfil its feeding requirements.

■ Water decalcified with oxalic acid

Another procedure entails the use of oxalic acid. Less dangerous to handle than nitric acid (although poisonous), it forms with calcium an insoluble salt, calcium oxalate, which precipitates and after a few hours appears as a whitish deposit in the tank. It produces water that is strongly decalcified, of about pH 6. The pH should be measured with indicator paper: if it is too high, a little acid (nitric or oxalic) may be added; if too low, it can be supplemented with a little caustic potash, rather than caustic soda, for the latter may overload the water with sodium. The ideal pH level is between 6 and 6.5.

WARNING

Never mix caustic potash and nitric acid directly. Clumsiness or carelessness in this respect may cause an explosion.

Watering

Whatever equipment is used and whatever the source of the water, it is essential that the latter should have been left lying for a while in a tank inside the greenhouse or room. The plants must never be allowed to suffer any shock as a result of the water being applied at the wrong temperature.

Watering with cold water, especially if repeated, is liable to be particularly dangerous. It will result in weakened growth, reduced resistance to disease and an overall delay in the vegetative cycle.

■ Storing water in the greenhouse

At one time it was customary to place a tray underneath the staging to catch any drops after watering the plants, but nowadays this is not advised because there is too great a risk of spreading bacterial and fungal diseases. Excess water should be allowed to flow directly onto the underlying gravel or onto the shade plants below the staging.

As previously mentioned, water may be stored beneath the ground level in the greenhouse itself, in two tanks, one for treatment and decanting, the other for distribution. A simple siphon is used to link one to the other, and the water is brought into the greenhouse by means of a pump furnished with a pressure control. If stored thus in darkness, the water is protected from any growth of algae. The tanks can be made from plastic or cement, but in the latter case, it is as well to line the interior walls with a waterproof resin.

If the reservoirs are not buried, they must be placed inside the greenhouse. Despite the encumbrance, particularly in a small greenhouse, this method has the great advantage of increasing the inside night time temperature of the greenhouse and reducing heat loss. The heat absorbed by the water during the day is partially released at night, provided, of course, the walls of the reservoir make this possible.

Epidendrum crassilabium. This species comes from Cuba and Costa Rica, and is also found in northern Brazil and Venezuela.

■ Watering techniques

Many automatic watering systems are available when building a greenhouse, but no matter how sophisticated they are, there is no substitute for the grower's own common sense. That is why they are not strongly recommended. If, for instance, you go away on holiday, the best solution is to call upon the assistance of a friend who also grows orchids.

In small greenhouses, nothing can replace the watering-can, which is the only method whereby you can meet the demands of each plant and prevent water stagnating inside the leaves (*Phalaenopsis*) or the flower sheaths (*Cattleya*). Watering with a low-pressure lance is also an excellent method, practical and precise.

There is only one right time for watering, and that is in the morning, no matter what the time of year. The fact that the water has time to evaporate throughout the day, combined with the higher temperature by day than at night, enables the roots to dry rapidly, without any risk of stagnant water, which may have serious consequences when the temperature falls at night. Watering must never be done in the evening or in the afternoon in winter. Leaves, sheaths and terminal shoots must be absolutely dry at nightfall.

In summer, afternoon watering must likewise be avoided, because of the strong heat. Watering provokes a temperature shock which causes the plant to open its stomata suddenly, thereby losing a large quantity of water through transpiration, even before the water just applied has time to be absorbed by the roots. The result, predictably, is that the plant wilts; and if this happens repeatedly, there is every likelihood that the orchid will not recover.

■ Frequency of watering

It is impossible to be too exact about the frequency of watering because there are so many options available, depending on many factors which the orchid grower will take into account, guided by experience, curiosity and intuition. For this reason, frequency of watering is seldom mentioned in horticultural guides dealing with orchids, apart from a generalized indication, such as 'abundant watering, tapering off in rest period', and the like. It is worth noting that 'abundant watering' can be interpreted variously as 'every other day', as in the case of a *Masdevallia*, or 'every week', as with an *Ansellia*.

Certain basic rules, however, can govern decisions as to frequency of watering:

- the higher the temperature and the stronger the sunlight, the more often will watering be necessary;
- a large container dries out much less quickly than a small one;
- an earthenware pot dries out more rapidly than a plastic pot;
- drying depends on the quality of surrounding air, its degree of humidity and its movement;
- the quality of the compost will play an essential role, notably in respect of drain-

Oncidium ornithorhynchum. This delicately scented species is from Mexico, Guatemala and Costa Rica.

age, the degree of decomposition, its compactness, its volume in relation to that of the roots, and its coarseness (the finer the grains, the better they retain water);

- the nature of the elements making up the compost is also important (some, like polyurethane moss, hold water well; others, such as charcoal, do so less effectively);
- a hanging plant, better aerated than one in a pot, needs watering more frequently;
- in large pots, the compost nearer the surface of the compost may be dry even though the underlying layers may be quite moist.

Humidification

Humidity is measured in hygrometric percentages of 0–100. Given that 100% corresponds to a saturated atmosphere, every application of additional water will result in condensation. The hygrometric percentage varies, of course, with temperature. The higher the temperature, the more water there will be in the air, in a gaseous state, for every hygrometric percentage point.

Where there are localized cold spots (e.g. on a pane or on a plant) saturation will be reached more rapidly, especially if the hygrometer rises above 80% in the centre of the greenhouse. So it is important to make sure that the hygrometer stays below this level, particularly in winter; otherwise there is a risk of a level of condensation that will have an adverse effect on the plants and, more especially, on the beauty of their flowers. Too high a humidity level can be remedied, according to the time of day, by ventilation or by raising the greenhouse temperature by 2–5°F (2–3°C). Excessive moisture makes the flowers more vulnerable to attacks of *Botrytis*, a fungus which develops in the form of a brownish-grey mould.

In a small greenhouse a satisfactory moisture level can be obtained by damping the ground and by giving a fine sprinkling to the leaves with a mister.

In a larger greenhouse, there are several systems designed to humidify the air. Tanks placed underneath the staging, open or closed, are comparatively ineffective, as is damping the floor, should the latter be of concrete slabs. To achieve a correct atmospheric humidity level, the surface of evaporation may need to be increased considerably. To do this, the paths should be lined with a thick layer of gravel which is watered daily. That is, in any event, very practical in avoiding the risks of falling on a concrete floor which may become slippery from water and, sometimes, microscopic algae.

Green plants placed under the staging also help to maintain a satisfactory level of humidity in the greenhouse. It is not a good idea,

Neofinetia falcata. This orchid, the only species of the genus, originates in Japan and Korea. By a remarkable phenomenon of convergence, it has evolved a form very similar to those of the *Angraecum* species.

however, to cover the work surface with gravel because this makes it difficult to clean and interferes with plant aeration.

Finally, there are two other procedures employed by professionals in large greenhouses: misters and cooling systems.

■ Misters

Designed to transform water under pressure into very fine droplets, misters are effective only if the greenhouse ventilation is right. They should not be used with tap water containing too much calcium, as this will lead to deposits on the leaves and the glass panes which cannot be removed.

Such a system can be made automatic. A humidistat hygrometer, set at mid-height, is linked to a timer which activates an electromagnetic valve controlling the flow of water under pressure in the misters. Other devices for measuring humidity are also marketed, each with certain advantages and disadvantages (price, accuracy and reliability). Hygrometers, simple and reasonably precise, are good value for money. They can also be regulated and maintained without many problems.

■ Cooling systems

In large greenhouses these are very useful for humidifying and cooling the interior during the summer, making it possible to grow plants with a maximum of light but without a rise in temperature.

Such a system requires an opening to the greenhouse at either end, one provided with a large ventilator for extracting the air contained in the greenhouse, the other furnished with a double screen filled with shavings or tiny pieces of polystyrene over which water flows. Air circulates in the interstices and blows into the greenhouse, with a rapid cooling and humidifying effect. Naturally, the area between the ends of the greenhouse must be absolutely airtight for the cooling system to function properly.

Maxillaria praestans. The *Maxillaria* are plants of the high forests of Central America, growing in Mexico, Honduras, Guatemala and Costa Rica.

Feeding

In 1878, the Comte du Buysson remarked, when describing his cultivation methods, that fertilizers best meeting the requirements of orchids should be 'colourless so as not to spoil the foliage and sufficiently strong so that when highly diluted, the water to be applied should not be clouded, whilst containing enough nutritive substances to produce an effect on the plants'. Peruvian guano came closest to satisfying these criteria: moreover, its very nature (bird droppings) made it an ideal choice, very near to the natural nutriment of epiphytic orchids in the wild. Having administered it in the ratio of 1 g to every litre of water during the period of vegetation, du Buysson pronounced it highly satisfactory. He also used, with success, ammonium carbonate in the same dosage.

Guano was for a long time utilized in agriculture for its high content of ammonium nitrate and phosphates. It is not surprising, therefore, that such a fertilizer should contain elements useful to 107 genera (or over 750 species) which du Buysson had grown. Unfortunately, when he spoke of adding solid manure to the pots, he omitted to mention either the composition or the procedure employed.

In due course improvements came about thanks to the use of dried blood, hoof and horn, or bone meal. The former was to be virtually abandoned because of its foul smell which lingers for several days after application, but hoof and horn or bone meal were recommended as basic fertilizers with a slow rate of decomposition; this was an important

attribute since repotting was carried out every other year, thus giving the fertilizer plenty of time to be released.

It is true, nevertheless, that during the first half of the present century, growers reacted very strongly against the use of fertilizer for orchids. 'Above all, no fertilizer', was the watchword for more than thirty years. Photographs of the time bear witness to the fact that this prevented the plants growing and flowering abundantly. In the light of our knowledge today, we are better able to appreciate the disappointments that growers of that time must have experienced. The uncontrolled use of fertilizer led regularly to the rapid death of the sphagnum moss and sometimes of the plant itself. For that reason, many growers gave it up; in most cases, at any rate, organic matter present in the compost, and sometimes in the water given to the plants, supplied the orchids with their nutritive needs.

Modern composts, made up of organic products which decompose very slowly, have made the application of fertilizer indispensable. Furthermore, the cultivation of orchids does not consist only of getting the plants to survive, but of exploiting all their potentialities and splendours. Correct feeding is one of the essential conditions for success.

Techniques

The fertilizers in use today are generally supplied in the form of a liquid. This is normally

Encyclia vitellina. The aim of every orchid grower is to bring out all the splendours and potentialities of the plants. Adequate feeding is one of the prime essentials.

applied in diluted doses which range from 0.2 to 1 g of liquid feed to every litre of water.

One essential point: on the evening before feeding, the plant must be thoroughly watered so that the compost and roots are rinsed clean, thus getting rid of any residual micro-crystals of fertilizer from a previous application. This operation requires a quantity of water almost three times the volume of the pot. Failing this, the undissolved fertilizer micro-crystals will join up and create zones of excess salinity, likely to scorch the roots, destroy the velamen, causing necrosis of the underlying epidermis, and kill the root. This phenomenon, at first localized, may quickly reach even the whole root system. Normally the roots absorb mineral and organic salts dissolved in the water used for feeding; but for reasons that need not be dwelt upon here, this absorption is only partial. The unabsorbed salts crystallize when the water evaporates. The speed and intensity of this crystallization depend, of course, on the evaporation, which is more marked in earthenware pots than in plastic containers. In the latter, evaporation occurs mostly on the surface of the compost; the moisture persisting at the base of the pot prevents the formation of the deadly crystals.

From the moment the root epidermis becomes cankered, the plant should no longer be fed with water or fertilizer. When it begins to look limp and the leaves start to crinkle, a common reflex, which leads to catastrophe, is to feed it, with the aim of restoring its strength. The last chance the plant may have to absorb some water through any epidermis that remains intact is thereby removed, because if the saline concentration of the compost is higher than that of the sap, water is quite unable to move from the outside to the inside of the root. The plant is doomed to die of thirst.

Solid fertilizers

The appearance on the market of 'slow-release' fertilizers aroused many hopes. These pellets or granules, mixed into the compost at the time of repotting, are supposed to release very gradually the nutritive substances they contain. Unfortunately, it does not always happen like that; as a rule, the elements dissolve much more quickly, and the length of time varies, moreover, from product to pro-

duct and from one application to another.

It is very difficult, too, to introduce, during the course of the year, variations in the composition of the fertilizers applied. But one cannot rule out the possibility of improvements in the years to come.

The composition of fertilizers

The objective of every feeding operation is to furnish each plant with the nutriment necessary to its development and physiology. These needs vary greatly, both in quantity and quality, according to the stage of the vegetative cycle: development of the roots, growth of the foliage, development of the inflorescence, flowers, fruits, etc. At each of these stages, it is important to supply base elements which best favour these natural processes, but to remain aware that some of them may have the opposite effect and prevent this or that phenomenon occurring. Thus too much nitrogen, given before or during the development of the inflorescence, may partially or totally inhibit flowering.

■ Macro-elements
Three elements, indispensable to orchids, must be given in large amounts. These are the macro-elements or major feeding elements, namely nitrogen (N), phosphorus (P) and potassium (K).

- Nitrogen is a major cellular source of proteins.
- Phosphorus is indispensable to the constitution of nucleic acids.
- Potassium is an essential ion in the composition of the intracellular medium of plant cells. It is involved in a variety of reactions, particularly those governing photosynthesis. A shortage of potassium leads rapidly to withering, an increase in transpiration and an arrest to cell division.

Alongside these three principal constituents, there are the so-called secondary elements and trace elements.

■ Secondary elements
The secondary elements, sulphur (S), magnesium (Mg) and calcium (Ca), although present in very small quantities in fertilizers, play a fundamental role. Sulphur is a major constituent of many proteins and is indispensable

Laelia gouldiana. Originally from Mexico, this orchid needs plenty of light.

to the synthesis of chlorophyll; a lack of it leads to severe chlorosis. Magnesium is the central atom of chlorophyll. Calcium and magnesium are to be found in the central layer of membranes. They are involved in enzymatic reactions, are antagonistic to other metallic ions (an excess of calcium, for example, means a deficiency of iron) and they play a role in cell permeability (absorption or elimination of water).

■ Trace elements

Just as necessary to the life of plants are trace elements which exist in the majority of commercial fertilizers: they are iron (Fe), manganese (Mn), zinc (Zn), boron (B), copper (Cu) and molybdenum (Mo). A lack of these may cause a variety of disorders and ailments. They do not participate directly in the building of tissue, but are primarily catalysts which, by their presence, engage chains of biological reactions. When these are complete, the trace elements are released and ready to activate further processes.

In the cultivation of orchids, the compost is so poor in nutritive substances and trace elements that it is essential to add the latter. Deficiencies may occur, and are not always easy to diagnose, but they can be prevented and cured. The same does not apply to poisoning (through excess), which is almost invariably serious, even fatal. As a result, it is important not to take chances in this area. Never, for example, try out a 'miracle' cure, but stick to the very satisfactory formulae recommended in the trade. Even so, the trace elements in fertilizer solutions are not always precisely listed on the package; nor is the list necessarily complete. So, to be on the safe side, it is as well to resort, over the course of the year, to feeds made by different firms.

Feeding throughout the year

At the risk of appearing dogmatic, it is safe to say that there are four principal periods in the feeding programme, which must take into account the following broad rules:

1 When new growth resumes, it is much more important to provide nitrogen than potassium and phosphorus. This is only logical, since the structure of plant tissue consists, in large measure, of nitrogen.
2 When flowering begins and the inflorescence develops, too much nitrogen may be inhibiting. So the formula goes into reverse: less nitrogen, more phosphorus and potassium. This is because the development and

Oncidium Bijou × *Odontoglossum uro-skinneri*, hybrid obtained by Marcel Lecoufle.

opening of the flowers entail a rhythm of cell division, and thus the formation of nucleic acids rich in phosphorus. Potassium, the major element of the intracellular medium and of metabolism of young tissue, is equally indispensable in this phase.

3 During the flowering period, a small level of nitrogen and phosphorus, and a high level of potassium must be maintained.

4 During the winter rest period, watering is reduced and totally halted; feeding should also be completely suspended or carried out at most once a month.

The feeding programme becomes rather complicated when a number of different genera are being grown. For certain orchids, the growth of the flower spike coincides with the growth of the leaf shoot, and it is impossible to separate the first two phases of the programme. The situation is further confused by the fact that if the compost contains a large amount of pine bark, the proportion of nitrogen has to be increased.

Many growers, refusing to be bothered with such a complex set of rules, have adopted a standard feeding method which suits the majority of epiphytic orchids:

● During the period of active growth and every fortnight, they apply a balanced fertilizer with a 20-20-20 formula, prescribed at the rate of 0.5 g per litre, namely a half-dose (the standard being 1 g/l), or 1 g for a 10-10-10 formula, which is the same.

● During winter (rest period), feeding is completely halted, or cut down by at least one-third or one-half, which corresponds more or less to the normal reduction in the rate of watering.

The rhythm of feeding is very variable according to different authorities and schools of thought. It may be done on an infrequent basis, e.g. 1 g to each litre of water applied between one and three times a month. Other people prefer to feed more frequently but with a more diluted solution, e.g. 0.1–0.2 g to each litre of water applied: this dosage avoids, as a rule, all risk of micro-crystallization, but nevertheless rinsing of the compost should be continued, even if only now and then.

An international code

The formula relating to fertilizers, which is regulated by an international code, is expressed by three numbers, e.g. 15-5-10, which means that the fertilizer in question contains, for every 100 kg and after combustion, 15 kg of N_2, 5 kg of P_2O_5 and 10 kg of K_2O. This formula is derived from nineteenth-century chemistry, and it is the one that still remains in use today.

Simple propagation

It is always useful to have several specimens of the same plant: it increases the size of a collection, makes it possible to exchange plants and limits the risks of losses through disease or accident. Apart from the relatively complex methods of multiplication based on cultures of embryonic tissue or raising from seed, there are various quite simple ways of propagating orchids, suitable even for the beginner. Almost all species can be raised by one or two of these methods, but it cannot be emphasized too strongly that they require the strictest aseptic preventive measures because of the potential trouble that may arise at the various stages of the proceedings.

Division of clumps

This is the most common method of simple propagation, basically applicable to sympodial orchids such as *Cattleya*, *Paphiopedilum*, *Miltonia*, *Masdevallia*, *Lycaste*, etc.).

Clump division has to be carried out at the time of repotting. This does not mean, however, that it should be done every time. It is essential to recognize the risks to which the plant is subjected, for there is a trauma attached to division as well as to repotting. The operation can only be practised on healthy, luxuriant plants. Moreover, many genera look more attractive when grown in large clumps (e.g. *Masdevallia*, *Miltonia* and *Paphiopedilum*). So this aspect also has to be borne in mind before resorting to division.

The flower quality is generally better on a large clump than on a smaller one. Therefore it is a good rule, particularly with *Cattleya* species, never to divide when there are fewer than three pseudobulbs on a single clump.

Once the plant is out of the pot and its compost has been carefully removed, it is possible to go ahead and divide the rhizome (the creeping stem to which the roots and pseudobulbs are attached). To do this, use a sharp bladed knife, previously sterilized in a flame. Then separate the roots, which is not usually a problem if they are not intertwined. The old roots, often rotten and perhaps hardly functional, should be cut off, at least partially. On the other hand, it is important to protect the new roots. If the right moment for repotting is chosen, the new roots will not yet be developed and so do not risk coming to harm.

If the roots form a compact interlaced mass (for example, *Cymbidium*) the only solution is to cut through the clump with secateurs. This is hardly in accordance with the aseptic conditions needed for such an operation, so extra precautions have to be observed after repotting.

The wounds caused by the cut must quickly be cauterized, either coated with a layer of grafting mastic or painted with an antiseptic solution. Before repotting, make sure the root system is clean and get rid of any remaining dead roots or leaves.

Watering should be suspended in the following days so as to allow the scar tissue to form properly. This is, in any event, the rule after any repotting operation.

The compost for repotting must be moist but not saturated. The surface may be sprink-

Keiki on inflorescence of *Phalaenopsis equestris*. Removal and repotting of keikis is a simple method of vegetative multiplication.

A technique for simple propagation: removal of the back-bulbs

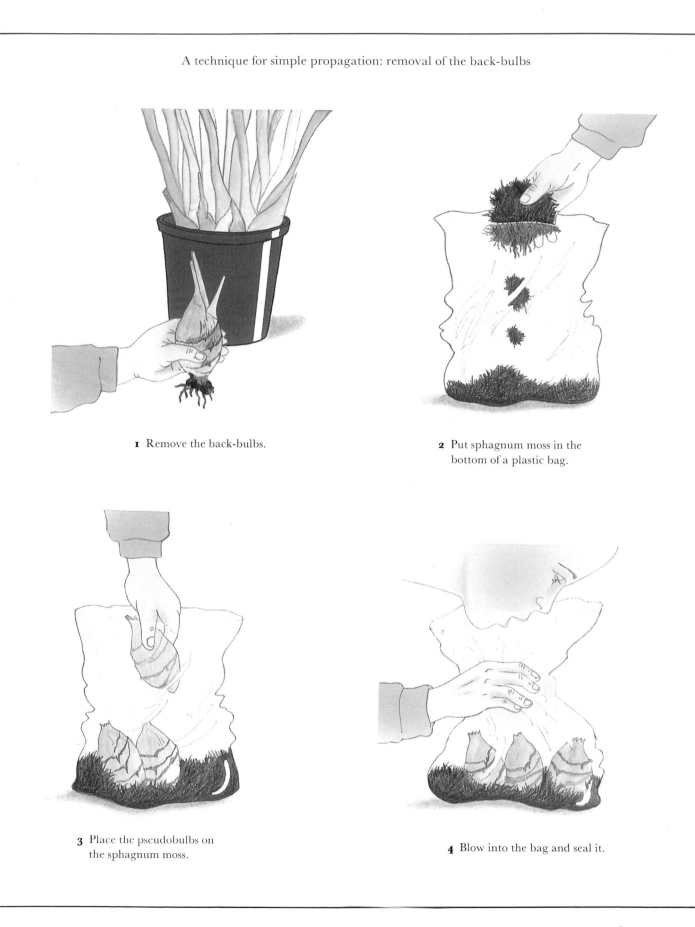

1 Remove the back-bulbs.

2 Put sphagnum moss in the bottom of a plastic bag.

3 Place the pseudobulbs on the sphagnum moss.

4 Blow into the bag and seal it.

led with water for the next few days in order to prevent drying out.

Removal of a back-bulb

As a rule, on a plant bearing pseudobulbs, only the ones at the front, which have sprouted the previous year, are likely to emit new shoots from which new pseudobulbs will develop.

The rear pseudobulb, known as the back-bulb, suitably treated, can give rise to a novel form of propagation. It is also possible to take two or three pseudobulbs from the same plant.

After cutting through the rhizome (taking the usual aseptic measures), each of the back-bulbs is scraped clean of root fragments which, with age, will generally have disappeared. This eliminates all risks of rotting or bacterial contamination. The leaves (or any remaining bits) should likewise be removed to avoid any excessive transpiration. The development of the new shoot comes from the dormant bud or eye at the base of the pseudobulb, utilizing the latter's water and food reserves.

Once isolated, the pseudobulbs are set on a layer of moist but not soaking sphagnum moss or river sand and placed in a fairly well-lit

position at a temperature of 68–72°F (20–22°C) and in a humidity of 70–80 per cent. A new shoot will then appear and develop within 3–4 weeks.

Alternatively, the back-bulbs may be placed on barely damp sphagnum moss inside a plastic bag. Before sealing the bag, blow in it to make sure the plants have plenty of carbon dioxide. Then hang the bag in a warm but shady part of the greenhouse. A few weeks later, depending on whether the buds were alive, new shoots will appear. When the roots begin to sprout from the shoots, open the bag and pot the plants. Keep the young and still delicate plants in frames in a shady and humid position for 6–8 weeks until they are growing strongly, and then repot.

This method of propagation demands a certain dexterity and carries some risk, in that there is a strong possibility of the plant rotting inside the bag. So you must supervise the whole process very carefully.

Removing the back-bulbs with a view to propagation is practical for a large number of sympodial orchids such as *Cymbidium*, *Oncidium*, *Odontoglossum*, *Catasetum*, *Zygopetalum*, etc.

Removal of keikis

Keikis (from a word of Hawaiian origin meaning 'babies') are young plantlets which develop either on a stem or on an old inflorescence. Although the propagation of keikis, by removal and repotting, is an extremely simple and satisfying method, the appearance of keikis is not necessarily a good sign. It may indicate that the plant or the part bearing them is getting old; or it may be a warning that something is amiss with the cultivation procedures. The appearance of keikis is associated with an absence or inhibition of flowering (except for certain *Phalaenopsis* species).

When the new roots appear, put the pseudobulbs in compost. When the shoots are sufficiently big, pot the plants.

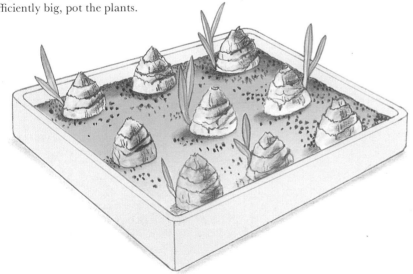

There are products on the market, in the form of paste, designed to induce the development of keikis; the results are not always convincing, particularly since such formations are also dependent upon season and temperature.

Keikis tend to form on many monopodial orchids (*Phalaenopsis*) and also on some sympodals (*Oncidium, Dendrobium, Thunia*, etc.).

In the case of *Phalaenopsis*, keikis can be encouraged to develop by wrapping a wad of moist sphagnum moss around three or four eye buds on the lower part of the inflorescence. The mother plant is then placed in the warm house. Under such conditions, all *Phalaenopsis* species will, sooner or later, develop keikis, the time lapse depending on variety, age of the inflorescence and growing conditions.

The keikis are removed when their roots are sufficiently long, say $1\frac{1}{2}$–$2\frac{1}{2}$ in (4–6 cm). They are then potted in a container suited to their size and in a compost identical to that used for the adult plant, but naturally finer grained.

Pruning

This method, which is suitable for long-stemmed monopodial species (*Vanda* or *Ascocentrum*) consists in cutting off the upper part of the plant, but naturally on the proviso that two or three aerial roots have already developed properly. The wounds are treated with antiseptic and the top part is potted in the usual compost.

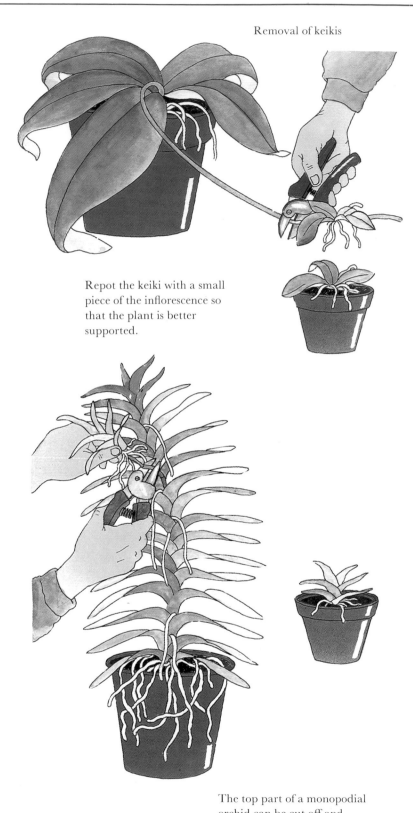

Removal of keikis

Repot the keiki with a small piece of the inflorescence so that the plant is better supported.

The top part of a monopodial orchid can be cut off and repotted. A very similar procedure is to remove and pot a lateral branch.

Cane cuttings

Certain orchids (*Dendrobium* and *Thunia*) possess long pseudobulbs in the form of canes, with many internodes. This strange structure can be used profitably for a method of propagation which is, in fact, simply a form of cutting.

At the time when food and energy stocks are at their highest, just prior to vegetative regrowth, one of the canes is removed and sliced into sections containing two or three nodes. These pieces are then laid horizontally in moist sand or, better still, live sphagnum moss; they are half-buried, with each shoot above the surface. The whole tray is put in a moderately warm greenhouse, under the same conditions as those for propagating back-bulbs. In this way the plantlets will grow and may be repotted after the same period of 6–8 weeks.

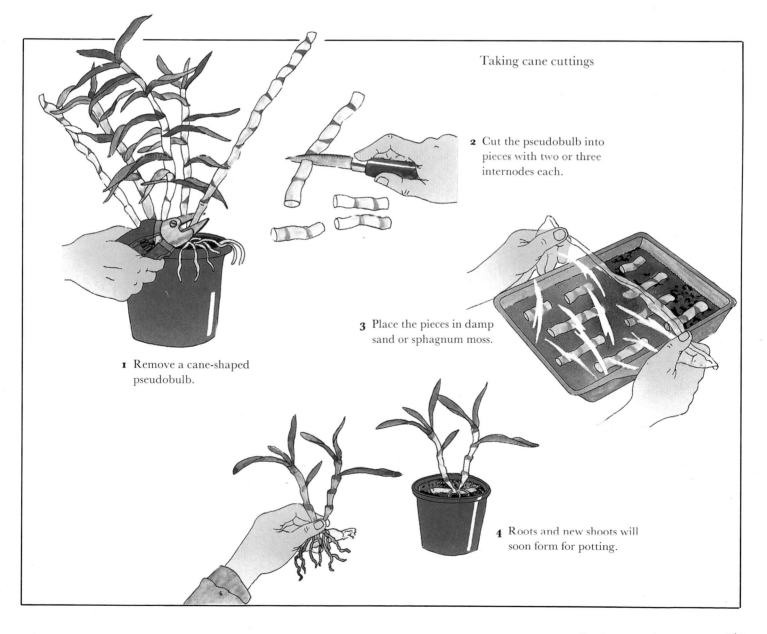

Taking cane cuttings

2 Cut the pseudobulb into pieces with two or three internodes each.

3 Place the pieces in damp sand or sphagnum moss.

1 Remove a cane-shaped pseudobulb.

4 Roots and new shoots will soon form for potting.

Seed raising

Botanists were for a long time puzzled as to how orchid seeds germinated. Deprived of all nutritive substance, the seeds were evidently incapable of germinating naturally except in close association with a fungus, *Rhizoctonia*, which brought the seed, and then the protocorm, all the nutrition necessary for the initial stages of development.

More than 150 years elapsed between the time orchids first began to be cultivated in the West and the complete mastery of the technique of raising seed in a flask. Scientific method took its cue from increasing knowledge and research into plant physiology. In 1799 Watcher achieved the first artificial fertilization, using seeds of a *Habenaria bifolia*. And in 1804 Salisbury sowed seeds in a pot which contained (or had contained) orchids, and recorded several germinations. Nevertheless, these experiments led to nothing. In 1826, Louis Noisette wrote in his gardening manual: 'It might be useful to sow seeds near the plants where they have been found', but his intuitive observation was not followed up.

In 1845, Scheidweiler and Neumann, noticing some young plants that had grown from seeds in pots containing other adult orchids, published, in the *Revue Horticole*, a paper that outlined the conditions necessary and sufficient for raising orchids successfully from seed. Soon afterwards, in 1848, Auguste Rivière induced seeds of *Epidendrum crassifolium* to germinate in the greenhouses of the Ecole de Médecine, confirming his success six years later. Unfortunately, because of serious disagreements with his patron, he was compelled to curtail his experiments.

In 1856 John Dominy achieved a breakthrough when he produced the first interspecific hybrid. The secret of his method, which was guarded jealously for many years, was to sow seeds obtained by cross-fertilization in pots of adult orchids. Until 1900 this was to be the only known and practised method of germination. Short-lived though it was, it can still be used by the beginner if great care is taken to ensure that the seeds are not washed away in the course of watering. To avoid this, it is best to immerse the pot briefly after laying a little sphagnum moss on top of the compost to prevent the seeds being dispersed.

In 1900, when Noël Bernard discovered the significance of symbiosis, his work led him naturally to the procedure of germinating seeds, in tubes containing cultures of specific fungi (*Rhizoctonia*) taken from the roots of adult orchids. This met with success. The method was practised by growers until the 1930s to obtain hybrids or to propagate species.

Bernard envisaged replacing this long and complicated operation with another technique, asymbiotic culture, i.e. without the aid of a fungus. The idea was simple: he believed, rightly, that the role of the fungus was not essential if one provided the seed with what the fungus itself supplied, namely sugar and mineral salts. Bernard's premature death in 1911 prevented further immediate progress in this field, but Louis Knudsen, in 1922, and Hans Burgeff, in 1927, perfected the culture media which bear their names and thanks to which it became possible to raise orchids from seed throughout the world. Since then, great improvements have been made to their composition.

Doritaenopsis Eclatant. Procedures for obtaining selected hybrids of exceptional quality are often possible only when techniques for sowing orchid seeds have been thoroughly mastered.

Pollination

This is the very first stage in the operation designed to create and obtain the seeds. In nature this is an extremely brief and complex procedure in which countless subtle strategies come into play in order to attract a specific insect, but in greenhouse cultivation it is astonishingly simply.

In the various genera, the central structure of the flower known as the column, which contains the sexual organs, displays a wide variety of forms, both in general and in detail. In every instance, however, the following elements are present:

- In the anterior part is a stamen separated into two, four or eight pollinia containing pollen in greater or lesser quantities, sometimes linked to a sticky pad, the viscidium. The pollinia are as a rule covered by an operculum (anther-cap), which moves easily at the slightest touch.
- Behind the pollinia is the rostellum, a lobe which prevents direct fertilization as the insect penetrates the flower.
- Farther back is the dome-shaped stigmatic cavity where the pollinia, carried from another flower by the insect, are deposited. It is worth noting that the structure of the column is always such that the pollinia are deposited by the insect as it withdraws, thus avoiding any risk of direct pollination.
- The ovary is situated in the lower part of the flower, beneath the sepals and petals. It forms a kind of stalk, which is transformed into a fruit after pollination; each fruit may contain several hundreds of thousands of seeds (up to two or three million in *Cycnoches*).

The technique of artificial pollination consists in transferring the pollinia into the receptive stigmatic cavity. To this end, it is necessary to use a small pointed reed twig, previously sterilized in a flame. The anther-cap is drawn back to reveal the pollinia which adhere to the reed when it touches their base. It is then easy to transfer these pollinia to the stigma of the same or another flower, simply by depositing them in the cavity. Although it is best to carry out this pollination on the spot, the procedure can be strung out for several weeks or months by keeping the pollinia dry and cool at 45°F (7°C).

Viruses are not, as a rule, transmitted by the seeds; but it is essential to remember that a virus may be transmitted to a healthy plant through the intermediary of pollinia from a plant affected by viral disease, whereas there is no problem in fertilizing a diseased plant with any kind of pollen (except in the case of bean yellow mosaic virus).

Successful fertilization is soon evident (though slower to appear in *Paphiopedilum*) from the withering of the perianth and the gradual swelling of the ovary. Ripening of the ovary may take several months, sometimes a year or more, depending on how developed the genus is (see the work of Y. Veyret).

It is advisable to observe the following rules:

- To carry out pollination, always choose a flower that has just opened. After the flower ages, the tubes of pollinia grow less readily inside the column and the ovary, so that fertilization is often only partial.
- Make certain that each subject is given a label with a serial number, cross-indexed to the names of the mother plant, the father plant and the date of pollination; this information is essential for the subsequent naming of the plants produced from the cross.
- Avoid soaking the stigma of the mother plant by clumsy watering. If necessary, the plant can be lifted and placed on an upturned pot.

Obtaining the seeds

Remove the capsules just before they burst open, testing for ripeness by pressing them lightly with the fingers. If the capsule yields to the pressure, it is suitable for use. Cut through the base of the stalk with a sterilized blade and pass the labelled capsule (provided it is not already open) rapidly over the flame of a spirit lamp; then cut the capsule with a sterile knife above a Petri dish, itself sterilized in the flame. This has to be done in a room free of all air movement, preferably in a sterile bucket or in a case with side openings large enough for the hands.

Once opened, the capsule releases the hundreds of thousands of seeds which can be stored for several months provided they are placed in dry surroundings at 45°F (7°C).

Pollination and fruit.
1 Sterilizing the rod in a flame prior to removing the pollinia.
2 Overall view of the flower.
3 Removing the pollinia.
4 Depositing the pollinia in the stigmatic cavity of another flower.
5 The ripe fruit.

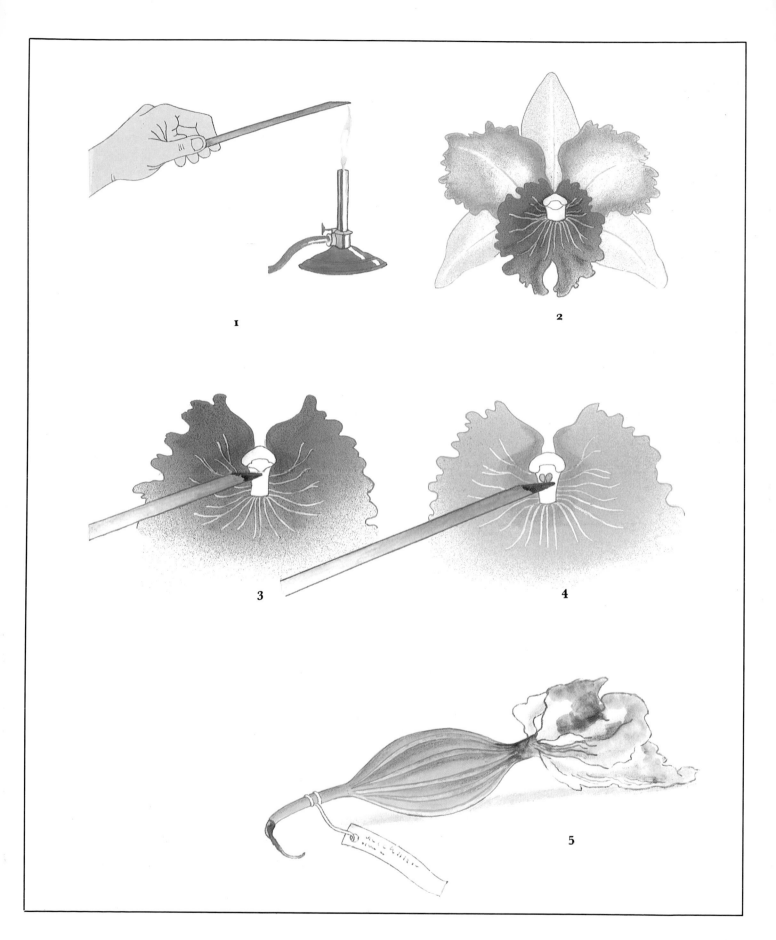

1

2

3

4

5

Preparation of media

A number of formulae are today proposed for specialized horticultural media, but the basic ones are those of L. Knudsen (solution C) and of Hans Burgeff. Others which include various organic ingredients are also used: tomato juice (Meyer formula), banana, peptones and fish emulsion (Tchang).

Each genus has its individual needs, so there is no universally applicable formula. These different media are prepared in the form of a gel, with the addition of 10–20 g of agar-agar to every litre of solution, dissolved warm in a little water. The pH should be between 5 and 5.5; this may be adjusted by the addition, drop by drop, of caustic ammonia or caustic potash in solution (to raise it) or of hydrochloric acid (to lower it).

The medium is divided up into suitable receptacles (glass phials, clear-glass whisky bottles, Erlenmeyer flasks, etc.) which are then sealed with a stopper pierced with an opening through which a small wad of cotton wool can be passed so as to permit aeration and gaseous exchanges during the culture, without risking contamination of the medium. The stoppered flasks are sterilized either in an autoclave, in a pressure cooker or (as is the modern tendency) in a microwave oven. The sealed flasks, after removal from the autoclave or oven, are placed on their sides so that the solution can solidify in the position which offers the greatest possible surface for germination of the seeds. It is advisable to wait eight days to be certain that the sterilization has been effective. The seeds can then be used safely over the following hours, days or months.

Sowing

If the seeds have been gathered aseptically, there is no need to disinfect them. Should that not be the case, or if the capsule is already

Removal and preparation of the seeds.
1 Removing the capsule, passing it briefly over the flame.
2 Opening the fruit.
3 The seeds in a Petri dish.

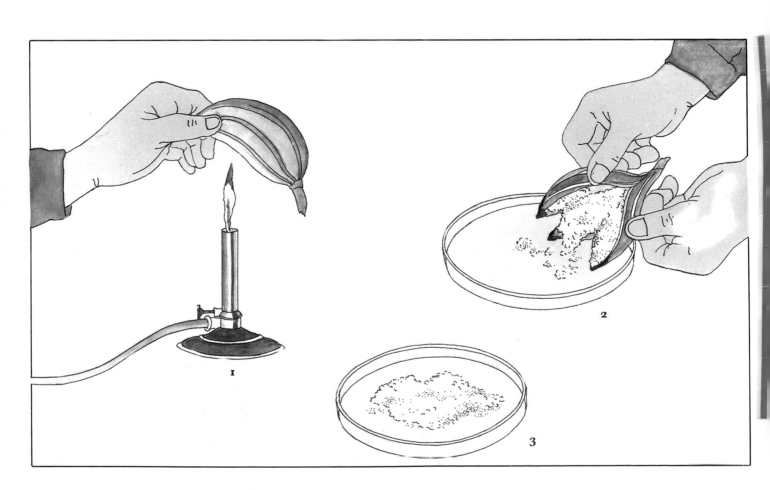

open, disinfect it in calcium hypochlorite, using the following method:

- Prepare the solution of calcium hypochlorite by dissolving 2.5 g of granules in 100 ml of distilled water; add two drops of household detergent (so that the seeds are thoroughly soaked).
- After twenty minutes filter the solution and divide into tubes.
- Put the seeds in the filtered solution and stir for two minutes; leave the tube standing upright for a minute.
- If the seeds settle at the bottom of the tube, empty the solution, keeping the seeds in the container. Should the seeds float on top, carefully tip the tube, allowing the liquid to flow between the thumb and the edge of the tube.

Thus disinfected, the seeds are dispersed in a little sterile distilled water, then sucked out using a syringe furnished with a large-diameter sterile needle, and injected into the flask. This simple method enables the seeds to be evenly distributed over the gel surface, with less risk of contamination.

Another, more traditional, method is to remove the seeds with a copper wire, the tip of which is flattened into the form of a blade. After sterilizing the blade in the flame and allowing it to cool, the seeds are lifted and placed in the tube, then sown on the gel simply by rubbing the surface. The neck of the flask and the stopper are disinfected in the hypochlorite before the flask is corked.

Pricking out

When the plantlets begin to develop inside the flask, they may be so numerous as to risk smothering one another. After taking the usual aseptic precautions, they can be pricked out into another flask, similarly prepared, in the same solution. Each plantlet will thus

4 Collecting the seeds.
5 Putting the seeds in a test tube.
6 Adding the hypochlorite solution.
7 Mixing.
8 Centrifuging.

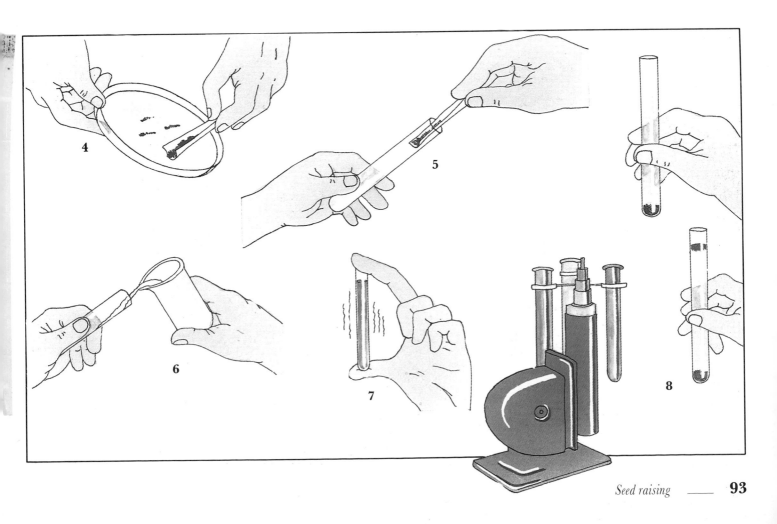

have all the space it needs to grow. Some months later a second pricking out may be desirable.

Light and temperature

The plantlets develop well at temperatures slightly above those that are suitable for adult plants. So flasks containing intermediate house orchids may be placed in a warm house, and cool house subjects in an intermediate house.

Where lighting is concerned, seedlings tend to behave in strange ways. It is best not to expose them to very bright light, and in certain cases deep shade is recommended, at least in the early stages. This applies to *Paphiopedilum*, which are plants of the undergrowth.

Repotting

When, after about six months or a year, the plantlets are sufficiently developed, they can be pricked out in seed pans which are placed in frames for several weeks. This operation is delicate and should cause as few traumas as possible. Do not try to take the plantlets out directly because the numerous roots are fragile and are likely to break.

The flasks have to be shattered in order to loosen the block of gel, which is then easily dispersed under a low-pressure jet of water at the correct temperature.

Separate the plantlets from one another and then prick them out in a pan in the same compost as is used for the adult plants, but with finer grains. Do not water them but sprinkle them lightly in the ensuing fortnight so as to keep the surface of the compost moist.

Removal and preparation of the seeds (continued).

9 Decanting the liquid.
10 Passing the spatula over the flame.
11 Draining the tube.
12 Passing the neck of the flask over the flame prior to opening.
13 Removing the seeds with the spatula.
14 Sprinkling the seeds over the agar surface.
15 The sown flask.

Steps **12, 13** and **14** have to be carried out under aseptic conditions (in sterile surroundings or inside a specially prepared box).

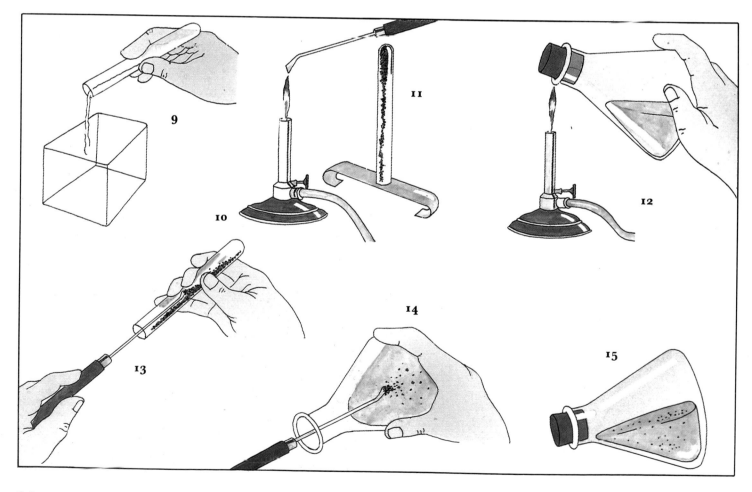

When the new roots appear, restore the normal pattern of watering and feeding.

Approximately two years later, on average, you can pot them individually, and in the next few years they should flower.

16 Flask filled with plantules.
17 Breaking the flask and washing away the agar in a jet of low-pressure water at 68°F (20°C).
18 Removing the plantlets.
19 Placing the plantlets in trays.

Pests, diseases and cultural ailments

It is profoundly upsetting when the orchid grower discovers that one of his favourite plants is affected by some ailment or disease. As in medicine, it is possible to make a diagnosis and to prescribe treatment. Nevertheless, the pathology of orchids cannot be reduced to a matter of simple prescriptions. Signs of wasting, whatever the causes and the symptoms, must be judged and interpreted in the light of the complex interactions that exist inside the greenhouse.

It is not always by accident that an insect or a fungal infection crops up in the course of cultivation. The great American orchid grower Walter Bertsch was among the first to take into account ecological factors inherent in greenhouse culture, in the prevention and treatment of bacterial and fungal attacks. This goes far beyond a remedy based simply on the prescription of a chemical product.

Of course, products designed to promote plant health have their rightful place, but they must be seen in perspective. It is always better to remove a few aphids found on an inflorescence by hand than to spray the buds, just ready to open, directly with an insecticide. Nor should such products, which are often dangerous, ever be used on orchids without calling to mind the warnings of Pierre Jacquet:

> The products in question are not as a rule authorized to be sold specifically for orchids, since such a use... has not been claimed by the manufacturer. As a result, the beginner has to take sole responsibility for the treatment and has no comeback against anyone in the event of his treatment causing damage to the plants.

Another consequence is that the labels do not give any instructions concerning their use on orchids, so it is always advisable:
— only to use the lowest prescribed dosage so as to avoid scorching, even if it means carrying out the treatment again after a few days should it not have proved entirely effective;
— to have available a spraying system with a nozzle elaborate enough to give out a very fine spray rather than large drops which are likely to cause scorching and dripping;
— to avoid spraying the flowers and flower buds, which are generally highly sensitive and liable to be covered with ugly marks, either from the colour of the product itself or from the damage to the flower tissues, which can become cankered.

Weeds

■ Algae

These may appear in the form of a thick green crust on the surface of the pot and on the roots. This crust is a barrier both to water and fertilizer, and it prevents the roots breathing properly. It may be a sign of poor air circulation, over-watering or the use of certain organic fertilizers (e.g. dried blood).

Remedies

The growing conditions (aeration, state of compost, frequency of watering) must be re-examined. Careful treatment can first be attempted with a highly diluted algicide detergent.

Algae make greenhouse pathways very slippery. It is possible to get rid of it temporarily by cleaning the paths with diluted disinfectant or an algicide detergent (taking care with the plants under the staging) and with suitable ventilation.

■ Oxalis

Yellow sorrel (*Oxalis*) is an extremely invasive plant which grows particularly in orchid compost and is likely to spread rapidly through the greenhouse (by fruit dispersal).

Remedies

It is essential not to use a herbicide and to remove the weed by hand. The most effective method is to get rid of it the moment it appears.

Oxalis. This weed has a marked preference for orchid composts, where it spreads rapidly.

Bacterial attacks

Whatever the origin, any attack of bacteria makes it imperative to observe the following rules suggested by Walter Bertsch:

- make sure there is enough air circulating;
- reduce the relative humidity in the greenhouse or in the section of greenhouse;
- keep the compost as dry as possible, according to the type of culture, until things are back to normal;
- transfer sick plants, provided they have been treated, into a section where the night temperature is 68°F (20°C) so as to obtain a strong shoot;
- increase the pH of the compost to 7 or 7.2 by applying dolomite lime, because many *Erwinia* (the bacteria that most commonly are to blame) do not appear to tolerate a high pH;
- apply a preventive fungicide twice a year to the plants, the staging and the supports; *Erwinia* (although a bacterium) also seems to be inhibited by fungicides;
- keep a watch for ground insects, particularly larvae, which are often vectors;
- remove all dead leaves from plants, pots, staging and ground;
- when watering, avoid water from one plant splashing onto another; this appears to be the principal way in which *Erwinia* infections are transmitted.

■ Bacterial rot

This ailment is due to a bacterium of the genus *Erwinia* or *Pseudomonas cattleyae*. It manifests itself as a large blister on the leaf, followed by rotting of the entire leaf.

Remedies

Cut out the affected part, taking care, while so doing, not to contaminate nearby plants or sappy material. Dust the wounds with a copper-based fungicide. Finally, to prevent the disease spreading, lower the temperature slightly and decrease the relative humidity.

Fungus diseases

■ Black rot of leaves and pseudobulbs

Dark spots appear at the base of the leaves and then turn black; they signify a more or

Bacterial rot.

less extensive necrosis which generally affects the pseudobulbs and the roots. This attack may be due to the presence and development of several fungi of the genus *Phytophthora*, spread by poor aeration, excessive humidity and too low a temperature.

Remedies

The rules laid down by Bertsch apply broadly to fungal diseases as well. If the plants are badly affected, the only solution is to destroy them. If the attack is only partial, remove the cankered tissues by cutting right round the infected zone (with a margin of about 1 in/2 cm) with a sterile knife.

Treat extensive wounds with a systemic fungicide powder.

Black rot.

■ Grey mould (*Botrytis cinerea*)

The perianth is dotted with small brown spots. *Botrytis* is a non-specific fungus which develops in condensing drops of water. The cause is condensation and relatively high humidity, together with a lowering of temperature.

Remedies

This is a matter mainly of prevention: raise the temperature to above 61°F (16°C) and lower the relative humidity. Affected flowers cannot be restored. A preventive treatment with an appropriate fungicide will make a further attack unlikely.

■ Basal and root rots

Pythium and *Phytophthora* are fungi which sometimes kill off young orchid plants when these are removed from the flask. On older plants, *Pythium* causes scattered spots to appear on the leaves, extending to the pseudobulbs. The back-bulb, often the first to be affected, turns black; gradually the other pseudobulbs become discoloured; this is a sign of invasion by the fungus which propagates inside the plant, through the rhizome, to attack the other organs. The cause of this rot is that the compost is too wet.

Remedies

Cut the affected back-bulbs off the rhizome, then cleanse by cutting towards the main bulbs until there is no further sign of internal necrosis. Cut an extra ½ in (1 cm) with a knife freshly sterilized for each section. Then treat with a fungicide. If the compost is too wet, suspend watering. If necessary, repot.

Botrytis cinerea on the flower of a *Phalaenopsis*.

Viruses

Irregular light patches appear on the lower and then the upper surface of the leaves. Hardly visible at the start, they develop gradually and lead to necrosis of old leaves. Discoloured or over-pigmented patches form on the flowers.

Such viruses are transmitted via the sap which contains viral particles. Careless handling (cutting flower spikes without sterilizing the instruments between plants) can lead to one plant contaminating another. There is some doubt as to whether insects such as cockroaches transmit viruses. It is important to

1

2

remember that a plant with a viral disease may not show any symptoms.

Remedies

So far no curative treatment has been discovered. The plant has to be destroyed, otherwise the entire collection risks being contaminated. Nevertheless, certain precautionary health measures can be taken: quarantine newly acquired plants, observe standard rules of hygiene, destroy insects which are potential vectors of viruses, and sterilize, in a flame or with a saturated solution of trisodium phosphate, every instrument used for maintaining the plant (especially for operations such as repotting and cutting flower spikes).

Viral infections on the leaves and flowers of a *Cattleya*
1 Appearance of discoloured areas on the flowers and leaves.
2 Appearance of necrotic zones on the flowers and leaves.

Basal rot as a result of a fungal infection of the rhizome and pseudobulbs of a *Cattleya*.

Pests

■ Springtails
These tiny whitish, wingless insects develop in the compost and cause it to decompose more quickly. They have no direct toxic effect on the plant.

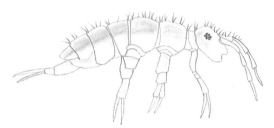

Remedies
Dust the surface of the pot lightly with a malathion-based insecticide.

■ Cockroaches
These insects, which reproduce rapidly throughout the year, do considerable damage in greenhouses, devouring, among other things, the very young leaves and flowers of *Phalaenopsis* during the night.

Remedies
To get rid of them (no easy matter, for they hide in cracks), set poisoned bait mixed with insecticide although unfortunately cockroaches are amazingly resistant to many insecticides.

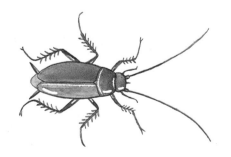

■ Aphids
The bites of these tiny, soft, slightly rounded insects, which live in colonies, cause deformation of the inflorescences and the flowers.

Remedies
Use an aphicide or insecticide preferably alternating various products.

■ Snails
The flowers and leaves are cut to shreds. Bites appear on the young roots.

Remedies
Scatter metaldehyde pellets over the surface of the compost. Take care to keep domestic pets away from the pellets.

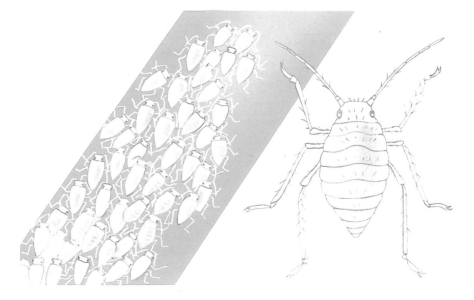

Opposite page, upper left: Springtail (much enlarged, ×20).

Lower left: Blatella germanica, one of the species of cockroach capable of ruining cultivated orchids.

Upper right: snails usually attack young plant shoots and parts of the perianth.

Lower right: a colony of aphids on a flower spike (much enlarged, ×5), and an enlarged aphid (×15).

Right: red spider mite (much enlarged, ×40).
Upper right: scale insect (×15).
Below: mealy bug (×15).

■ Scale insects and mealy bugs

The upper side of the leaves and the folds are covered with tiny immobile insects enveloped in a white powdery substance (mealy bugs) or in a shield (scale insects). Adult scale insects, attached to the plant by their mouthparts, do not move. But the very young larvae, in their exploratory stage, are highly mobile and spread everywhere. They are so tiny as to be

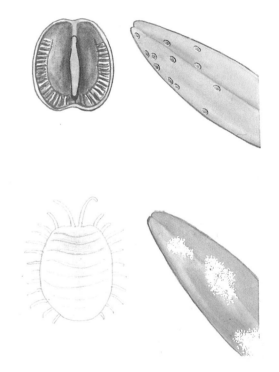

virtually invisible, especially on *Cattleya* where they find an ideal refuge under the parchment-like sheath.

Remedies
Speedy action is needed. If only a few plants are involved, simply touch each insect with the point of a brush dipped in an insecticide or methylated spirits. With bigger collections, several successive treatments may be required with a malathion-based insecticide. The signs of success are when the insects start dropping off.

■ Red spider mites
The symptoms take various forms. Large greyish patches may appear on the young leaves, especially on the lower side, of *Lycaste* and *Cymbidium*. Alternatively, there may be small rough areas on the buds. When the attack is severe, the flowers show deformed growth.

Such are the reactions of the plants to the bites of these mites as they feed (virtually identical to those caused by aphids).

Remedies
These mites thrive in a warm and dry atmosphere, and are discouraged by high atmosphere humidity (but not so high that fungi become a problem). Infestations should be treated with an acaricide.

Cultural ailments

■ Roots outside the pot

The cause of this is simple neglect. Repotting should have been carried out several months ago. The roots will also protrude from the container if the compost is too highly compressed.

Remedies

Repotting is a matter of urgency, and all the roots outside the pot must be cut away. Any attempt to replace them in the compost, given their length and fragility, would lead to them breaking and thus entail risks of infection. A satisfactory compromise, however, is to cut them down to about 6 in (15 cm) and then return them to the compost.

Roots growing out of the pot.

■ Dead roots

There may be many causes; too much water, prolonged drought, fertilizers that are too concentrated, failure to rinse the compost prior to repotting, use of soft or treated water, etc.

Remedies

Remove all the dead roots and repot in fresh compost, gradually resuming the sprinkling and later, when the new roots appear, normal watering.

■ Wrinkled pseudobulbs

This is caused by excessive dryness or necrosis of the roots.

■ Leaf scorch from the sun

Dry, cankered, black (generally white-bordered) patches appear on the central or most exposed portions of the leaves. The reason is too much sun, insufficient or no shading, or even a faulty cooling system.

Scorching of leaves by sunlight.

■ Leaf scorch from pesticides

This comes about as the result of using the product in the wrong concentration, applying an unsuitable product or mixing two incompatible products.

Remedies

Read the instructions on the label very carefully; experience teaches prudence in this area. Try out a small quantity before treating all the plants. Moreover, if applying two products, use them in turn at intervals of several days rather than mix them.

■ Shrivelling of leaves

This ailment, which only seems to affect *Oncidium*, is due to temporary dehydration when the shoot appears, associated with irregular watering.

Remedies

There is no curative treatment. The leaves tend to go soft in time. As a precaution, it is important to keep the compost properly moist and to ensure that the young *Oncidium* are not subjected to alternate phases of drought and humidity as they grow.

■ Reddening of leaves

A red pigment on the upper surface of the leaves indicates excessive lighting, poor root condition, insufficient nitrogen in the feed or a combination of these different factors.

Remedies
Reduce the lighting, improve the condition of the roots and compost, and apply a balanced fertilizer.

■ Yellowing of leaves
If the whole leaf turns uniformly yellow, it is a sign that the plant is in distress. The causes are various: excessive lighting, repotting done badly or at the wrong time, lack of nitrogen, ageing, destruction of roots by over-watering, or temporary cooling.

It is worth remarking that this condition may be normal for orchids with deciduous leaves just before they fall (*Calanthe*, *Catasetum*, *Pleione* and some *Dendrobium*).

Sap and sooty mould.

■ Guttation
Guttation is a frequent phenomenon in *Cattleya* and *Cymbidium*. At the moment of flowering, a sugary droplet is exuded onto the inflorescence at the attachment of the ovary; this substance is rich in nitrogen and calcium salts, and very attractive to ants.

The significance of this guttation is debatable; is it a sign of over-watering, which causes the plant joints to crack, or is it a normal phenomenon, to which many exotic orchids are accustomed in nature, whereby plants and ants live in close conjunction?

In the greenhouse one consequence of guttation is a kind of sooty mould. When the droplet is too big, it falls on to the foliage where it forms an ideal substrate for a particular type of fungus. Large blackish marks then appear on the upper side of the leaves. These can be cleaned off easily with water supplemented by a little detergent, and are not poisonous to plants.

■ Fall of flower buds
During their development, the buds turn yellow or reddish, then become cankered and drop off. The causes may be too much heat or poisoning of the plant by ethylene. Even a small concentration of ethylene is highly toxic and it may be given off by a faulty gas burner, by brush fires, by a bonfire lit too close to the greenhouse, by proximity to a main road or by poor ventilation in the greenhouse.

Remedies
Make sure the thermostats are working, ventilate the greenhouse properly and do not allow faded flowers to remain on the plants because they exhale ethylene.

■ Premature drooping
This may be a symptom of the plant being poisoned by ethylene, but it is a normal condition when fertilization occurs (except in *Paphiopedilum*).

Cultivation of orchids

Coelogyne ochracea. This species is grown in the cool or intermediate house; it needs absolute rest in winter.

Brassavola glauca. *Brassavola* have been hybridized with *Cattleya*.

Orchids long enjoyed the reputation of being plants that were virtually impossible to cultivate. Today things have gone to the opposite extreme. Indeed, some growers will assert that orchids are difficult to kill off. This is not entirely true, but indicative of the changes that have come about in the last century or so.

Many orchids have proved strongly resistant to stressful conditions such as excessive heat, comparative cold and drought, but only so long as these are temporary. In the short term, therefore, they may be sufficiently tough to withstand adversities of various kinds. Yet in time they become increasingly vulnerable and it is very easy to kill them off; all you need to do is over-water them or expose them to inadequate light or unsuitable temperatures. So long-term survival is the real challenge, the crucial test of the grower's skill. The better the care, the healthier the plants: given correct feeding, a change of compost at the opportune moment and preventive treatment against viruses, bacteria, fungi and insect pests, orchids will respond in full and rewarding measure.

Britain was the first major importer of exotic orchids but it took almost fifty years (the first half of the nineteenth century) before the country lived down the reproach levelled against it by Joseph Hooker, director of Kew Gardens, as having been, during that period, 'the grave of tropical orchids'. And the path to progress was strewn with all manner of preconceived, not to say mythical, notions which had to be swept aside before John Lindley, the pioneer of orchid growing, could declare with confidence (1838) that 'these plants must be grown in conditions as near as possible to those of their natural surroundings'.

Once the beginner is familiar with the climatic, environmental and nutritional conditions of a particular orchid in its original habitat, there need be no problems of cultivation. In certain cases, where little or nothing is known of these natural conditions, the cultivated plant may well die within two or three years; but such species are not normally marketed. They are likely to include orchids from Europe, from temperate regions of the southern hemisphere and North America, and *Coryanthes* species, which beginners cannot keep alive for more than three or four years.

Nevertheless it is possible – in many instances – to keep a single plant in cultivation almost indefinitely: one vegetative shoot will succeed another year after year and in principle there is no reason why the process should ever stop. Some specimens in Kew Gardens are more than 120 years old. Unfortunately this cannot be said of many orchids in the Paris Natural History Museum which died in the winter of 1948 for lack of heating fuel after having come through the war without any trouble.

In certain respects the growing of orchids has something in common with data processing. The laws of evolution have 'programed' them in such a way that their biological processes and hence their very lives correspond to the data concerning the outside surroundings to which they have adapted. The program can only be changed as it is fed with adequate data, which in this case includes:

- variations of day/night and annual temperatures;
- surrounding humidity;
- intensity and daily duration of lighting;
- duration of rest period.

Epidendrum prismatocarpum. This species is cultivated, like the majority of *Epidendrum*, in the intermediate or warm house.

One advantage of dealing with a living organism rather than a machine, however, is that no matter how rigorous the programming, there is always some permissible give and take when it comes to ideal conditions. Thus a multitude of genera and species which have similar needs can be kept together under the same greenhouse roof. The data-processing analogy therefore only takes us so far. In orchid cultivation, apart from the general directives that apply to a genus as a whole, much emphasis is to be placed upon intuition and to the perception of an individual plant's actual needs from day to day.

This book obviously cannot describe the cultural requirements of the 730 known genera and 25,000 species belonging to the Orchidaceae. But the information that accompanies the following plates, dealing as it does with basic principles, should enable the beginner to grow and successfully maintain the majority of the epiphytic orchids that are commercially available. Results cannot, of course, be achieved only by intuition; they depend, too, largely on experience, on knowledge about places of origin, and on observation and analysis of the structure, form and behaviour of each individual part of the plant.

In any event, a book that purported to deal with the cultivation of all orchid genera could hardly fail to be repetitive. In 1961 Mr and Mrs Dunsterville took an inventory of all the species found on an old tree that had recently died and fallen to the ground. The tree itself was not exceptional, having grown in a Venezuelan forest at an altitude of 4200 ft (1300 m). The authors were thus astonished to come across forty-eight species belonging to fifteen different genera. This observation, like so many others, shows to what extent identical ecological conditions may bring together a large number of genera belonging to various tribes and subtribes. Naturally, if ecological conditions are identical, so too ought to be the cultural conditions.

From another point of view, however, it is worth mentioning that certain very diversified genera, such as *Oncidium* and *Dendrobium* harbour a number of subgroups which exhibit the most varied ecological and cultural needs. Thus horticultural criteria do not necessarily coincide with those employed by botanists in their determination of genera. Several genera may be cultivated by the same method; and, conversely, a single genus may be cultivated in a number of ways.

So although there must inevitably be certain redundancies in the following descriptions, they are as a rule limited to genera that are closely related and with similar or almost similar requirements.

Gongora truncata. This orchid is cultivated, like *Stanhopea*, in a hanging container.

Angraecum Bory
and ANGRAECOID ORCHIDS

Tribe: Vandeae   Subtribe: Angraecinae

Bory de Saint-Vincent described and named the genus *Angraecum* in 1804, from the Malay word *angurek*, used by the natives to designate similar types of epiphytic orchids (notably *Aerides* and *Vanda*). In due course other Madagascan and African orchids were discovered and at first incorrectly assigned to this genus; they included *Aerangis, Aerides, Rangaeris, Tridactyle* and *Jumellea*, most of which are amenable to methods of culture quite similar to those for *Angraecum*.

This very large genus contains more than 200 species distributed over much of Africa: tropical southern Africa, South Africa, Madagascar and the neighbouring islands.

The pale white, sometimes ivory-flecked, flowers bloom in winter. They are pollinated at night; and this is precisely when, in order to attract the pollinating insect, many *Angraecum* give out an extraordinarily heavy scent which is in itself good reason for growing these plants.

The flowers, often with a very long spur, are sensitive to shocks or even slight touching of the petals, especially at the edges. They often have a thick,

almost leathery, texture which enables may of them to remain in bloom for several weeks. This exceptionally long flowering period is an adaptation to the relatively rare appearances of the pollinating insect. It increases the chances of pollination quite considerably, though perfectly in accord with their ecological needs.

The *Angraecum* are relatively tolerant plants and quite easy to grow.

Angraecum eburneum. A species originally from the islands of the Indian Ocean. The superior position of the lip gives it a very unusual appearance.

■ Light

The *Angraecum* are not really shade plants. In nature they are frequently subjected to alternating shade and full sun; in culture a compromise can be effected by giving them very little shade in winter and from 50 to 100 per cent during the hottest hours of summer.

■ Temperature

The *Angraecum* are either warm house subjects to be grown at 59–75°F (15–24°C), representing winter night and summer day temperatures respectively, in the case of low-altitude species, or intermediate house plants in the case of mountain species. But practically all of them are sufficiently tolerant to be grown in the intermediate house, the few exceptions including *Angraecum magdalenae*, which has to be cultivated in the cool house.

The *Angraecum* species differ, in fact, as to their optimal temperature requirements, obviously depending on the climate of their zones of origin. Provided other cultural conditions are respected, they can survive fairly wide variations of temperature level. This is not the case with other related genera such as *Aerangis*, for which the comparatively strict recommended temperatures must be observed.

■ Humidity and watering

Angraecum are plants of continuous growth with vegetal activity which simply slows down in winter. They appreciate fairly high surrounding humidity of around 70 per cent, which implies that they need perfect ventilation. In winter the humidity level can be much lower, in the order of 40–50 per cent.

The plants should be generously watered during the most active period of growth (March to October) and much more moderately in winter. In summer occasional spraying is sufficient to maintain satisfactory moisture levels.

plants of varying size	long flowering period
flowers perfumed only at night, grown according to species in the three types of greenhouse	moderate light, although not shade plants
	high surrounding humidity (and thus good ventilation)
no rest period; simply suspend watering in winter	repot every other year, in spring
simple propagation by removing and repotting shoots	reputedly easy to cultivate in greenhouse, more uncertain indoors

■ Feeding

This should be carried out once a fortnight from March to October, using a balanced fertilizer in normal doses of 0.5–1 g per litre. Suspend feeding in winter.

■ Repotting and compost

Repotting must be done in spring, at the beginning of the active growth period. Modern composts, which are constituted of tree fern fragments, osmunda and pine bark, entail repotting every three or four years.

Small *Angraecum* are repotted with the same ingredients, the measure of the grains being consistent with their size.

Large *Angraecum* need bigger pots, which give them better stability, and many species may also be grown on rafts.

■ Propagation

Like many monopodial orchids, the *Angraecum* throw out shoots furnished with roots; as soon as the latter are 4 in (10 cm) long, they can be removed and repotted.

Angraecum leonis. Discovered by Léon Humbolt around 1880, it comes from Madagascar and the Comoro Islands.

Angraecoid orchids which can be grown like *Angraecum* species:
Aeranthes; Aerides; Aerangis; Cryptopus; Cyrtorchis; Diaphananthe; Jumellea; Oeonia; Oeoniella; Tridactyle.

Most suitable temperature conditions for various Angraecoid orchids (according to Joyce Steward):

— **Cool house:** *Diaphananthe; Angraecum magdalenae; A. conchiferum; A. sacciferum; A. montana; A. mystacidii; A. thomsonii*

— **Intermediate house:** *Jumellea; Diaphananthe; Tridactyle; Cyrtorchis; Angraecum compactum; A. soronicum; A. erectum; A. calceolus; A. germinyanum; Aerangis bradycarpa; Aerangis citrata* var. *rhodosticta; Aerangis ugandensis.*

— **Warm house:** *Cryptopus; Oeonia; Oeoniella; Aeranthes; Angraecum distichum; A. eichlerianum; A. infundibulare; A. eburneum; A. giryamae; A. sesquipedale; Aerangis biloba.*

Ansellia
Lindley

Tribe: Cymbidieae   Subtribe: Cyrtopodiinae

This genus comprises two species: *Ansellia africana* and *Ansellia gigantea*. Some authors claim that the former is merely a variety of the latter, in which case the genus would be reduced to a single species with an extremely broad area of distribution embracing much of southern Africa from the western equatorial region to the whole of the south-east. With such a large range there is considerable polymorphism: there are, in fact, numerous varieties of the type species.

Ansellia africana is also known as the leopard orchid, because of the colour of its perianth and its spotted appearance. It is a very beautiful plant of large dimensions (about 5 ft/1.5 m) and certainly cannot be raised in a small greenhouse. A sympodial orchid with cylindrical pseudobulbs topped by half a dozen large leaves and a terminal, often branched, inflorescence, it bears numerous delicately scented flowers. The flowers are of very long duration, appearing either in spring or summer, on the pseudobulb formed the previous year.

■ **Light**
Ansellia need strong light, but not direct sun.

■ **Temperature**
It is a warm house plant.

■ **Humidity and watering**
During the period of growth, *Ansellia* need a high level of surrounding humidity (70 per cent); during the rest period, 50 per cent is sufficient.

Watering should be generous throughout growth. Considerable quantities of water are necessary to supply enough moisture for the large container used. Development of the root system and the heavy consumption of water at this time limit the risk of root rot. But successive waterings should be well spaced out.

During the rest period, when the new shoots have reached maturity, watering should be suspended and the compost merely sprayed from time to time so that it does not dry out completely.

■ **Feeding**
Apply a 20-20-20 type fertilizer twice a month during the growth period.

■ **Repotting and compost**
The standard compost is made up of pine bark, pieces of tree fern and osmunda in equal parts.

Repotting is normally carried out every two years.

■ **Propagation**
By clump division when repotting.

Ansellia africana is the only species of a genus with a wide distribution through tropical Africa. There are numerous varieties of this orchid.

large plants: about 5 ft (1.5 m)	long flowering period
warm house	strong light, but not direct sun
period of winter rest with occasional spraying of compost	repot every other year
simple propagation by clump division when repotting	reputedly easy to grow in warm house
cannot be grown indoors	numerous flowers

Bulbophyllum

Thouars

Tribe: Epidendreae   Subtribe: Bulbophyllinae

Aubert du Petit Thouars described and named the genus in 1822 in his monograph on the *Orchidées des Îles Australes d'Afrique; Bulbophyllum* signifies 'bulb-shaped leaf', a description which could equally apply to many other genera. With more than 2000 known species, it is today the biggest genus in the orchid family. Its area of distribution is equally extensive, covering all the intertropical zones of America, Africa and the Indo-Pacific region. Some authorities assign *Cirrhopetalum* and *Megaclinium* to this genus.

Not all *Bulbophyllum* species are of equal horticultural interest. Some have tiny flowers, often without any particular beauty; and many give out an unpleasant, even putrid, smell.

Bulbophyllum do not lend themselves much to hybridization, and are more highly esteemed by lovers of rare, exotic plants than by the majority of collectors who tend to be attracted by the dazzling and sensuous colours of the more celebrated horticultural genera.

Although the general appearance of the inflorescence is highly varied, all *Bulbophyllum* species possess an extraordinary articulated lip which is sensitive to the slightest touch. Its function is to unbalance the insect as it lands, sending it tumbling against the column underneath by means of a subtle rotating movement. The insect's back makes contact with the pollinia and carries them unwittingly to another flower.

All *Bulbophyllum* have a rapidly growing horizontal rhizome from which a series of angular pseudobulbs develop, each bearing a single thick, leathery leaf (hence their name). The flowers are borne on a long stem emitted from the base of the pseudobulbs; they may be arranged in umbels (*Cirrhopetalum*), situated on either side of a horizontal blade (*Megaclinium*), divided into a spike or in the form of a single flower (*Bulbophyllum*).

Both the flowering period and its duration vary considerably according to the species.

All *Bulbophyllum* are reputed to be tolerant and easy to cultivate.

warm house or intermediate house plants	the wide variety of geographical origins imposes diverse methods of watering (regular, suspended or curtailed in winter)
very variable dimensions; from 1 in (2 cm) to 2 ft (60 cm)	
reputedly easy to grow	plants dislike being repotted (every three years)
moderate light	best grown in hanging container

■ Light

This should be moderate. *Bulbophyllum* like a good deal of shade.

■ Temperature

These orchids are grown mainly in the warm house, but some species, such as *Bulbophyllum lobbii*, should be raised in an intermediate house.

■ Humidity and watering

In summer, during the active growth phase, the surrounding humidity level should be high (about 70 per cent), with good ventilation. It can be less (50–60 per cent) in winter.

Watering methods vary according to species. Obviously, with such a vast genus and so many geographical origins, there can be no uniform recommendation. Certain species come from regions where there is a dry season (China, Burma, Himalayas), in which case these conditions must be reproduced in cultivation, at least for several weeks, so that the pseudobulbs can mature properly. Other tropical species observe no rest period and should be watered regularly all year round. And others are somewhere in between, so that watering needs to be spaced out during winter.

■ Feeding

Twice a month with a half-dose of a balanced 20-20-20 fertilizer during the period of strong vegetative growth.

■ Repotting and compost

Bulbophyllum can be grown in a flat pot, fixed or hanging, or suspended on cork bark or a tree fern raft. They do not like being repotted and often need several months to recover, so it is advisable to take the most careful precautions with this operation. In order to limit the frequency of repotting, which should ideally be only once every three years, choose a compost which does not decompose too quickly, e.g. 30 per cent tree fern, 40 per cent pine bark, 20 per cent expanded polystyrene and 10 per cent polyurethane moss, plus dolomite lime at the rate of 3 g per litre.

Naturally, any sign of decomposition will necessitate immediate repotting, for which there is no particular season unless there is a definite rest period.

A broad, shallow, flat-bottomed container allows plenty of room for the frontal bulb and this will reduce the risk of escape from the pot.

■ Propagation

By clump division when repotting.

Bulbophyllum elastissinatum.
Bulbophyllum is the largest genus of orchids in terms of species, which number about 2000.

Calanthe

Robert Brown

Tribe: Arethusease   Subtribe: Bletiinae

It was in the course of his voyage to Australia in 1821 that Robert Brown discovered and identified this genus, which he named *Calanthe*, from the Greek *kalos* ('beautiful') and *anthos* ('flower'). There are 150 known terrestrial species, most of them originating in South-east Asia, Japan and the islands of Melanesia. Several species are to be found in the central African region and one only (*Calanthe mexicana*) in Central America.

The plants are relatively sturdy and undemanding. There are two kinds, corresponding to two types of climate, and therefore requiring two methods of culture.

- The *Calanthe* with deciduous leaves possess pseudobulbs from the base of which an erect flower stem, varying in length from 8 in (20 cm) to 3 ft (1 m), develops; they originate in tropical regions with a long dry season.
- The *Calanthe* with persistent leaves, possessing no pseudobulbs, with a shoot that stems directly from the rhizome, are from temperate or warm countries with no marked dry season.

All the species, nevertheless, have a number of common features, so that broad recommendations for cultivation may be followed.

■ Light
Calanthe thrive on fairly bright light but not full sun, which scorches the leaves.

■ Temperature
The species with bulbs should be grown in a warm house, and those with persistent leaves in an intermediate house.

■ Humidity and watering
All *Calanthe* need a high surrounding level of humidity, constant in the case of those with persistent leaves, spring and summer only for those with deciduous leaves, which should be placed during winter (period of absolute rest) in a dry, cool spot, at 50–54°F (10–12°C).

Calanthe with persistent leaves must be watered regularly during their phase of active plant growth. Then, when the leaf shoots are adult, watering should be reduced for several weeks but without allowing the compost to dry out. Normal watering is then resumed only after flowering.

Deciduous species should be abundantly watered while they are growing, but given complete rest during the winter. Between these two periods and before the leaves fall, watering should gradually become less frequent until the flowers appear at the beginning of winter, after the leaves drop.

Calanthe Harrissii. This hybrid with pseudobulbs and deciduous leaves flowers in early winter.

■ Feeding

This is useless if the compost contains leaf mould. If not, apply a half-dose of a balanced fertilizer every fortnight while the shoots are developing.

Feeding should be totally suspended in winter for deciduous-leaved species and reduced for persistent-leaves species.

■ Repotting and compost

Calanthe with deciduous leaves need repotting in early spring and those with persistent leaves in late spring. This can be done annually or every two years, using plastic pots of greater width than height, because the roots of *Calanthe* tend to develop mainly at the surface.

Species with bulbs may be treated as follows: remove them from pots in winter, some weeks after flowering, place the pseudobulbs in a dry, cool place, at 50–54°F (10–12°C), until early spring, then repot.

All the plants like well-drained soil, the composition of which varies according to the author consulted:

- a rich compost, consisting of a mixture of leaf mould and fresh soil (M. Lecoufle);
- lava grains, weathered granite, vermiculite and expanded clay, used on their own or in mixture, together with 10 per cent sphagnum or leaf mould.

The addition of leaf mould rules out feeding, but more than 10 per cent will make the compost too heavy, with consequent risks of water retention and thus root rot.

Some authors (Rittershausen) recommend placing dried cow-dung at the bottom of the container.

■ Propagation

By division of clumps (pseudobulbs or leaf shoots) when repotting.

Calanthe veratrifolia. Lacking pseudobulbs and with persistent leaves, this species has a long flowering period of several months.

Calanthe with persistent leaves	Calanthe with deciduous leaves
flowering: spring	flowering: early winter
light: bright but not full sun	light: bright but not full sun. Semi-shade in winter
temperature: intermediate house	temperature: warm house (spring, summer), cool house (winter, 50–68°F/10–20°C)
humidity: high, over 60 per cent	humidity: high during plant growth; dry in winter
watering: about every other day during growth phase. Three-week interval after flowering. Every 5–10 days in winter	watering: identical pattern during growth phase. Reduction and then complete suspension in winter
repotting in early spring: annual or every two years	repotting in late spring: annual
cultivation: reputedly easy	cultivation: reputedly easy

Cattleya Lindley and LAELIINAE

Tribe: Epidendreae   Subtribe: Laeliinae

These orchids were so named, in 1824, by John Lindley, in honour of William Cattley, collector of exotic plants and the first to grow them successfully in Britain. Cattley, in fact, had been attracted by the orchids' strange, leathery leaves and the pseudobulbs with which some other plants had been packed for their journey from their country of origin, Brazil. He proceeded to pot them, giving them heat and humidity, and was surprised a few months afterwards, to witness the appearance of beautiful and delicately scented mauve flowers.

Nowadays the orchid is so familiar that it is difficult to appreciate the excitement which it initially aroused. For the experienced grower and beginner alike, it constitutes a reference and basic model for the cultivation of many other epiphytic orchids. Species of *Cattleya* are distributed over virtually the entire tropical part of Central America and several countries in South America.

Two kinds of *Cattleya* are distinguished: the so-called bifoliates, with pseudobulbs bearing two leaves, and the unifoliates, with a single leaf. The orchids of the latter group, of which *Cattleya labiata* is a representative, have big flowers and a very large lip; the bifoliates have smaller flowers in greater number and with a firmer texture; the lip, too, is smaller.

For more than a century horticulturalists have used a dozen or so *Cattleya* species to obtain a large variety of hybrids. Crossing species very freely, both with one another and with those of related genera, growers have brought striking improvements to the quality of the flowers:

- the use of *Laelia* species has been responsible for a better texture and the introduction of a vast range of colours;
- the contribution of *Brassavola digbyana* is to be seen in the development of the lip, with elegantly folded or fringed borders;
- the brilliant red coloration is due to *Sophronitis coccinea*.

More recently, particularly successful crosses have been obtained with *Broughtonia*, these hybrids being notable for their harmoniously proportioned flowers.

The nomenclature of hybrids combines the names of their parents, e.g. *Laeliocattleya* or *Brassolaeliocattleya*. When an intergeneric hybrid contains three genera or more in its parentage, it is given a proper name, e.g. *Potinara*, after Félix Potin, the famous early twentieth-century grower, the antecedents of which include species of *Brassavola*, *Cattleya*, *Laelia* and *Sophronitis*. Matters can be further simplified by naming hybrids after the initials of their parental genera: *Lc* for *Laeliocattleya*, *Blc* for *Brassolaeliocattleya*, etc., or by giving them an abbreviation of their intergeneric name (*Pot.* for *Potinara*).

Today there are hundreds, indeed thousands, of recognized cultivars, in an immense range of subtle, harmonious and contrasting colours, and an equally wide variety of perfumes. It is rather a pity that the latter quality is not greatly appreciated by growers nor accounted as of much importance by competition juries. Some scents are admittedly repellant, but others are wholly captivating. Strangely, in the case of *Cattleya*, the same perfume enjoyed by one person may be loathed by another; so much so that it is hard to describe or appreciate *Cattleya* by their scent alone.

■ Structure

Cattleya are sympodial plants with pseudo-bulbs fairly close to one another. These are 4–8 in (10–20 cm) long, thicker in the centre than at the ends, sheathed by a leaf and surmounted by one or two thick, coriaceous leaves from the base of which develops the inflorescence; the latter is protected during its early growth stage by a sheath.

Each year, three shoots generally appear at the base of the front of the pseudobulb formed in the previous year, and from these shoots one or two new pseudobulbs develop.

■ Flowering

The season is variable. Most *Cattleya* develop a new shoot in spring. Some bloom immediately, the flowers emerging from the sheath while it is still green. Others have a shoot which ripens in summer, producing a sheath within which the inflorescence grows slowly and flowers in late winter or even in the following spring. Such a lengthy maturation period usually results in the sheath fading and withering, so that it can easily be removed. Watering must be done with care so that no water collects inside, which may carry a risk of rotting.

Yamadara Midnight 'Magenta'. *Yamadara* is a genus consisting of quadrigeneric hybrids, created by crossings of *Brassavola, Cattleya, Epidendrum* and *Laelia*.

Orchids requiring the same care as *Cattleya*
Brassavola
Laelia
Rhyncholaelia
Broughtonia
Sophronitis, although hybridized with *Cattleya*, are grown in the cool house, whereas their hybrids (e.g. *Slc*) are cultivated in the intermediate house.

intermediate greenhouse plants	large size: 20–80 in (50–70 cm)
scented flowers (especially unifoliates)	indoor cultivation inadvisable
need plenty of light	very sensitive to heat, especially direct sun
marked variations of day/night and seasonal temperatures	nocturnal lighting has an inhibiting effect on the flowering of certain groups
repot every other year, in spring, when root shoots appear	flowers last 10–15 days on average
restrict watering in autumn and winter	plants prone to attack by scale insects

Cattleya
Lindley and Laeliinae

Tribe: Epidendreae
Subtribe: Laeliinae

■ Light

Cattleya need good and plentiful light all year round. The leaves, however, must not receive any direct sunlight, which by reason of excessive heating would cause necrosis by scorching; the measure of heat can be tested by feeling the leaf. Insufficient light is a major reason for *Cattleya* failing to flower. The colour of the leaves is a reliable indication of the plant's reactions:

- dark green – not enough light;
- pale green or olive-green – normal light;
- yellow – sign of root necrosis and imminent death.

Shading, always from the outside of the greenhouse, is necessary when the sun is shining strongly. It should be adjusted seasonally, regionally and according to personal intuition. The more accustomed the plant becomes to shading, the greater is its sensitivity to heat from the sun. Only if a cooling system is introduced is it possible to expose the plant to sunlight.

It is worth remembering that some species of *Cattleya* and certain Laeliinae react to nocturnal lighting by failing to flower; this makes it difficult or even impossible to grow them indoors.

■ Temperature

Cattleya are grown in the intermediate greenhouse, for which the term 'cattleya house' has long been synonymous. In fact, the temperature should never exceed 82°F (28°C); and in winter it must not fall below 59°C (15°C). For successful flowering there has to be a marked temperature contrast from day to night and from season to season. As a general rule, too, the following temperature preferences should be observed:

Cattleya bicolor. Originally from Brazil, where it was discovered in 1836, the species is bifoliate.

Laeliocattleya Puppy Love 'True Beauty'. Almost all the unifoliate *Cattleya* possess a strong musk-like perfume. The scent of Puppy Love is especially captivating.

Laelia anceps. Originally from Mexico and the eastern part of the Andes range, *Laelia* are very often hybridized with *Cattleya*, to which they contribute their dazzling colour (*below, right*).

- yellow *Cattleya*, descended from *Cattleya dowiana*, do not like low temperatures;
- red *Cattleya*, with *Sophronitis coccinea* or *Laelia* species among their ancestors, do well under low temperatures of 50–54°F (10–12°C).

Such tendencies, however, do not warrant a change of greenhouse. All *Cattleya* can thus be raised in an intermediate house; any slight differences of temperature inside the greenhouse may be exploited so as to find the most suitable positions for the individual plants.

■ Humidity and watering
During their most active growth phase, *Cattleya* thrive at a relative humidity of 60–80 per cent. The higher the temperature, the higher the humidity, this being achieved by watering the greenhouse pathways, spraying the leaves and the compost, and ensuring proper ventilation.

These orchids are very sensitive to overwatering. Make sure, therefore, particularly if they are planted in large containers, not to water them (with certain exceptions) more than once a week. In autumn or after flowering, reduce the frequency of successive waterings, if necessary to only twice a month. The surrounding humidity is also reduced during this period to 50–60 per cent.

■ Feeding
After carefully rinsing the compost, feed with a half-dose of 20-20-20 fertilizer once a fortnight during plant growth and once a month in winter. Adjustments should be made in the application of food according to the composition of the substrate (especially with pine bark) and the growth cycle.

■ Repotting and compost
It is essential to choose the right moment for repotting, which normally coincides with the very start of root growth, in spring, and the swelling of the buds from which the root shoots will develop. There is thus no risk of damaging the young roots. It is a serious mistake to repot when the roots have already grown or when the plant is actually in bud.

Repotting should be carried out every other year, using black plastic pots. As for all sympodial orchids, the plant should be positioned off-centre so as to leave sufficient room for the frontal bulb. This is particularly important for *Cattleya* which have

Cattleya
Lindley
and
Laeliinae

Tribe: Epidendreae
Subtribe: Laeliinae

a strong tendency to overflow their containers. There is no need, however, to choose an over-large pot. For procedure when the roots protrude from the container, see page 102.

In the case of a very large clump, it may be necessary to consider dividing it into two or three smaller clumps. When doing this, the following rules must be observed:

● keep more than three bulbs in each clump;
● sterilize the knife before each cut;
● check the condition of the rhizome section for possible bacterial or fungal infection.

Repotting is carried out as follows:

● begin by lining the bottom of the pot with some fairly large pieces of expanded polystyrene or washed gravel to improve drainage;
● set the plant in a thin layer of compost so that the rear part touches the edge of the pot; the rhizome should be lightly covered by the compost;
● heap up the compost but take care not to crush the plant;
● finish by giving the plant a support, such as a bamboo cane set alongside the rhizome, which will enable the pseudo-bulbs to be kept upright with plastic ties attached to the base of the leaves. Staking has the triple advantage of helping the plant to take root, giving it a more attractive appearance and saving space in the greenhouse.

After repotting, suspend all watering for three weeks. Only the leaves will need light spraying (see page 74).

One of the most common growing media consists of 60 per cent pine bark, 25 per cent expanded polystyrene, 15 per cent polyurethane moss, and an addition

Cattleya guttata var. *leopoldii*. Quite widely distributed in Brazil, the *leopoldii* variety is often regarded by botanists as a distinct species of *Cattleya*.

Laeliocattleya Betty Cake. This recent hybrid was obtained, as with all *Laeliocattleya*, from a crossing of *Laelia* and *Cattleya*.

Broughtonia sanguinea.
Broughtonia, recently crossed
with Cattleya, bring
astonishing shapes and
colours to their hybrids.

Cattleya Sir Jeremiah Colman
'Blue Moon' AM/RHS
HCC/AOS. The beauty of
this hybrid is sufficient to
explain the awards it has
received.

of dolomite lime, at the rate of 2 g per litre.

■ Ailments to which the *Cattleya* are prone

Black rot
This is revealed by the colour of the pseudobulbs, which first turn brown and then black. The symptom shows that the plant tissues have been invaded by a *Phytophthora* fungus. Carry out treatment as soon as possible (see page 97): cut out the affected parts, soak in a fungicide solution and repot.

Absence of flowers
There may be several causes: insufficient light, a late-flowering species, or a fertilizer containing too much nitrogen, which encourages plant growth to the detriment of flower development.

Blackening and necrosis of the sheath
This is the result of water stagnating between the base of the sheath and the leaf. If, as a consequence of inadequate watering, this stagnation is prolonged, the stalk and flower buds will canker in their turn. The sheath must therefore be cut off, partially or wholly, to remedy the situation.

Viruses
Cattleya are especially prone to viruses which damage their flowers, often in spectacular fashion: colour breaks, spots, pigmentation faults and cankers. There is no known remedy at present. The best solution is to burn the plant and take proper preventive measures (see page 98) to ensure that the viruses do not spread to the entire collection.

Chysis
Lindley

In 1834 John Henchman, collector for the firm of Low, discovered *Chysis aurea* in the Cumanacoa valley of Venezuela. The *Chysis* species, and particularly *Chysis aurea*, are reputedly among the most beautiful orchids of Central America. They are epiphytic plants which originated in Mexico and the northern regions of South America, growing at an altitude of around 5550 ft (1700 m).

A recent revision of the genus has led botanists to conclude that there are two species of *Chysis*, not six, as had been formerly claimed. All *Chysis* are thus varieties of *Chysis bractescens* or *Chysis laevis*; *Chysis aurea* is therefore a variety of the former species.

Crosses with related genera (*Phaius* and *Calanthe* in particular) are rare; virtually nothing is known about their phylogenetic affinities.

The appearance of the pollinia, more or less fused into a single mass, is the origin of the generic name (Greek *chysis* = melting).

Chysis orchids have very thick, almost succulent, petals and sepals, which gives them a fairly long flowering period of about two weeks. They are sympodial plants with long fusiform pseudobulbs and large deciduous leaves which fall, partially or entirely, in autumn. The inflorescence develops from the lower part of the new pseudobulb and grows at the same time as the latter.

The whole plant (pseudobulbs and inflorescence alike) tends to adopt a pendulous habit, and this can be remedied by the use of a suitable support. Many people, however, prefer to cultivate *Chysis* species in perforated hanging baskets; this has the dual advantage of retaining their natural habit and supplying them with better ventilation and lighting.

Chysis bractescens. This is one of the two species of the genus *Chysis*, which comes from the mountain regions of Central America.

■ Light

Chysis are not shade plants, but care must be taken not to expose them to full sunlight, which scorches their leaves. They thrive on fairly bright light, which is a further strong argument for growing them in hanging baskets.

■ Temperature

Chysis are cultivated in an intermediate house or warm house during their vegetative growth stage (spring and summer). In winter (the rest period) they need to be kept cooler; the cool section of the intermediate house is ideal.

An important prerequisite for success is to maintain a sharp difference between day and night temperatures during the growth period, thus reproducing the climatic conditions of tropical mountain plants.

■ Humidity and watering

The humidity level should be high during vegetative growth; watering, too, needs to be generous, with a partial drying out between each application.

As for all deciduous leaved orchids with strong pseudobulbs, winter is a rest period when watering should be almost totally suspended. Light intermittent spraying will prevent excessive withering of the pseudobulbs.

■ Feeding

Since the vegetative part develops at the same time as the inflorescence, many growers do not trouble to apply selective feeds according to the phases of the growth cycle. They simply feed their *Chysis* two or three times a month with a balanced fertilizer. Naturally, these feeds must be suspended during the rest period.

■ Repotting and compost

The frequency of repotting depends on the nature of the compost and the containers. With a hanging basket, the imbalance may be such that repotting becomes necessary each year. With a pot and adequate support, repotting can be done at much longer intervals, e.g. every three or four years; the pseudobulbs, clustered against one another, take a long time to overflow.

The best time for repotting is at the very start of plant growth, when the new root shoots are just appearing.

potentially large plants, 24–28 in (60–70 cm)	natural pendulous habit
flowers in early summer	total rest period after leaf drop
intermediate or warm house in summer	intermediate or cool house in winter
cultivation in pots or hanging baskets: propagation by clump division	strong lighting but no direct exposure to sun

Among various compost formulae, two are particularly favoured by growers:

- a mixture of tree fern fragments, pine bark and charcoal, in equal proportions;
- a combination of washed gravel, charcoal and coconut fibre, again in equal proportions.

Some growers prefer more traditional methods and pot their *Chysis* in the compost used for *Cattleya* species.

A long rest period and the use of a compost that does not readily decompose will, in certain cases, restrict the necessity of repotting to every four or five years.

Chysis laevis × Chysis bractescens var. *aurea*. This famous cross produced legendary hybrids which have now vanished. (Recent specimen obtained by Marcel Lecoufle.)

Coelogyne
Lindley

Tribe: Coelogyneae   Subtribe: Coelogyninae

Lindley was the first to describe and name this genus, in 1822, after a specimen of *Coelogyne cristata*, collected in Nepal by Dr Wallich in 1822. The genus *Coelogyne*, which includes a large number of species, comes from the Greek: *koilos*, hollow, and *gyne*, female.

There are approximately 125 species in the genus *Coelogyne*. Their distribution extends from India, southern China, Thailand, Vietnam and the rest of South-east Asia to Java, Borneo, the other islands of Indonesia, New Guinea and northern Australia.

These sympodial plants possess globular pseudobulbs, their size varying according to species, with two coriaceous, persistent leaves. The inflorescence is borne by the new shoot which develops on the rhizome, on the lower part of the pseudobulb of the previous year. In most species this shoot eventually becomes a new pseudobulb. The pseudobulbs may be close together, almost linked, or they may be far apart from one another, all the way along a creeping rhizome which soon escapes from the pot.

■ **Temperature**

Originally from low, medium and high altitudes, *Coelogyne* species may thus be grown in each of the three types of greenhouse:

Cool house	Intermediate house	Warm house
C. corymbosa	C. barbata	C. asperata
C. cristata	C. carnea	C. dayana
C. elata	C. chloroptera	C. flexuosa
C. fimbriata	C. cumingii	C. foerstermanni
C. flaccida	C. fuliginosa	C. mayeriana
C. nitida	C. graminifolia	C. miniata
C. mooreana	C. huettneriana	C. odoratissima
C. ochracea	C. lawrenceana	C. pandurata
	C. lentiginosa	C. rhodeana
	C. massangeana	C. rochusseni
	C. nervosa	C. rossiana
	C. ovalis	C. sanderae
	C. parishii	C. sparsa
		C. speciosa
		C. sulphurea
		C. testacea
		C. tomentosa
		C. viscosa
		C. venusta

(from *Encyclopedia of Cultivated Orchids*, Hawkes)

Light

Coelogyne species need strong lighting but never direct sunshine, which would scorch their leaves. If they are not given plenty of light they have the tendency, through a compensatory mechanism, to develop large, very dark green leaves, to the detriment, naturally, of their flowers.

Humidity and watering

Warm house *Coelogyne* orchids are grown without a rest period, with a constantly high humidity level and in a thoroughly drained compost. It is important to ensure that water does not get inside the new shoots, otherwise they may rot.

Cool house species need an absolute period of rest, from the time the pseudo-bulbs complete their maturation to the resumption of plant growth in spring.

In all cases, the surrounding humidity must be kept close to 60 per cent, together with good ventilation.

Feeding

This should be monthly during vegetative activity. The same pattern should be followed, all year round, for warm house *Coelogyne* species. Use a balanced fertilizer in half-doses, at the rate of 0.25–0.5 g per litre.

Repotting and compost

Two compost formulae are particularly recommended:

- a mixture of pine bark, sphagnum and charcoal in equal proportions;
- a mixture of tree fern, osmunda and charcoal, also in equal proportions.

Coelogyne orchids do not respond well to repotting; sphagnum moss does not tolerate fertilizers, and many species quickly escape from the pot. These factors complicate the situation. Certain species need to be repotted every year, others every two or three years, the right moment, of course, being at the resumption of plant growth.

Epiphytic cultivation on a tree fern raft gives excellent results, and they may equally successfully be grown in hanging baskets.

Propagation

This is done by clump division when repotting. Never isolate a clump containing less than three bulbs.

very variable size	may be cultivated under the three standard temperature conditions (cool, intermediate and warm house) which thus determine their other cultural requirements: watering, total (cool house) or partial (intermediate house) rest period, fertilization
plants like light but not full sun	
not responsive to repotting	
extremely variable flowering period	genus very seldom hybridized

Coelogyne rhodeana. The species comes from Burma, Thailand and Kampuchea.

Coelogyne virescens. The genus *Coelogyne* comprises about 100 species, found throughout South-east Asia.

Cymbidium

Swartz

Tribe: Cymbidieae   Subtribe: Cyrtopodiinae

In 1799 the Swedish botanist Olof Swartz described and named the genus *Cymbidium* (from Greek *kymbes* = boat), referring to the shape of the lip. The *Cymbidium* species are terrestrial plants growing at high altitude, originally from South-east Asia, the Indonesian islands and northern Australia. There are approximately seventy species from which thousands of hybrids have been created.

At the beginning of the present century these orchids were immensely successful and extensively marketed, but recently they have lost much of their former prestige. Nevertheless they are still cultivated widely in Europe and the United States. In fact, it is rare for a genus to unite so many horticultural qualities: exceptionally long-lasting flowers (on average two months), vigorous growth, comparative ease of cultivation, a great variety of forms, colours and sizes, and a relatively inexpensive price.

Some *Cybidium* originally from Indonesia have to be raised in the warm house. They are: *Cymbidium aloifolium*, *C. dayanum*, *C. lancifolium*, *C. pendulum*, *C. pubescens* and *C. simulans*. Certain species originating in Taiwan or neighbouring climatic regions need to be grown in the intermediate house. Those that come originally from high-altitude regions, such as the Himalayas or Burma, are cultivated in the cool house, as are the vast majority of large-flowered hybrids. The latter can be grown as half-hardy subjects in many temperate and mountainous regions.

Cymbidium Indian Tea 'Superlative'. This hybrid shows the influence of *Cymbidium lowianum* in its green perianth and purple lip.

Light

Cymbidium need good light throughout the entire year. This is absolutely essential to good flowering. In this context, careful inspection of the leaves provides a reliable indication as to what corrections of light may be necessary:

- if they are soft and dark green, the light is insufficient;
- if they are relatively firm, of good texture and light green, the lighting is right;
- if their tips are turning red or black, they are getting too much sun; but this is also a sign of drought, necessitating an immediate increase in the frequency of watering.

In the greenhouse, where the temperature rises very rapidly and where evaporation occurs more slowly than in the open air, some shading must be given during the summer; as well as sufficient aeration and ventilation.

In temperate countries, when it is warm during summer, *Cymbidium* may be grown outdoors, provided they are sheltered from strong sun around midday, which may scorch the leaves. It is not so much the sun itself which does the damage as the resultant heating of the leaves. If such heating is counteracted in the greenhouse by a cooling system, *Cymbidium* can withstand direct sunlight.

Temperature

These cool house plants have very special temperature requirements. They may, occasionally or for brief intervals, be able to withstand extreme temperatures of over 95°F (35°C) or under 35°F (2°C). So it is possible, in temperate latitudes, to bring the *Cymbidium* out in late spring and take them in towards the end of summer. But at the hottest times of day they need shade and plenty of water so as to maintain a high level of surrounding humidity.

Cymbidium Sensation 'Chianti'. The horticultural qualities of *Cymbidium* make it one of the ten genera most frequently hybridized and most highly prized by collectors.

large plants, long flowering period	cool house subjects, apart from certain botanical *Cymbidium*
strong light, but direct sun (if it results in excessive heating) may scorch the leaves	can be raised as half-hardy subjects (outdoors in summer) in temperate regions; cooler conditions needed in late summer/early autumn to induce flowering
restrict watering and suspend feeding in winter	high level of humidity and hence good ventilation
repot every two or even three years	simple multiplication by clump division when repotting
easy to cultivate in cool house and with cooling system	temperature requirements not compatible with indoor cultivation

Cymbidium
Swartz

Tribe: Cymbidieae
Subtribe: Cyrtopodiinae

Rather than seeking an unvaried ideal temperature, the grower would be well advised to consider two types of temperature variation in order to achieve satisfactory plant growth and obtain good flowers. Given an average temperature of around 55°F (13°C) in winter and 68°F (20°C) in summer, *Cymbidium* need a variation of 10–13°F (6–7°C) from day to night. This difference is absolutely essential to get the flowers started; it is equally essential, in order to induce flowering, to give them a night temperature of between 43 and 53°F (6 and 12°C), when their pseudobulbs are mature, for a period of three or four weeks.

This balance is achieved naturally in temperate zones of the northern hemisphere when *Cymbidium* are placed outside in the first and second weeks of September and then brought into the greenhouse around the end of that month. Development of the inflorescence and flowers will only come about if the nocturnal temperature does not exceed 59°F (15°C).

These conditions must be observed throughout the winter months until the plants are brought out in early summer.

■ Humidity and watering

Cymbidium, being partly terrestrial plants, have roots that differ from those of most purely epiphytic orchids. For one thing, their roots are best kept constantly moist, and for this purpose plastic pots are far preferable to earthenware pots which because of their porosity cause water to evaporate more quickly.

Cymbidium do not, as a rule, observe a rest period and must therefore be watered plentifully throughout the year, with the compost allowed to dry out between each

Cymbidium greenhouse (Vacherot et Lecoufle). A cooling system such as this is ideal for the cultivation of *Cymbidium*, but the standard conditions offered by a cool greenhouse suit the majority of these orchids.

Cymbidium dayanum. Unlike most horticultural *Cymbidium*, this species can only be grown in an intermediate or warm house (*below, right*).

Cymbidium Starbright 'Capella', AM/AOS. This recently obtained hybrid has a luminous beauty which justifies both its name and the award it received from the AOS.

application. There are, nevertheless, two exceptions to this rule:

- Newly repotted *Cymbidium* go through a delicate period because of possible traumas and injuries to the roots during this operation. The application of too much water at this stage could cause scarring and pave the way for bacterial and fungal infection of the roots;
- In the case of certain botanical *Cymbidium* (e.g. *Cymbidium devonianum* Ldl. & Paxt.) watering needs to be severely restricted in winter, with just enough water provided to prevent the bulbs and leaves withering. A rest period follows the maturation of the pseudobulbs and lasts until the inflorescence appears in spring.

These orchids must be grown in a moist atmosphere; the hotter it is, the higher the humidity. In such conditions raising the humidity level prevents excess loss of water through transpiration.

■ Feeding
See general advice, page 77 *et seq.*

■ Repotting and compost
Since the beginning of the century a number of growing formulae for *Cymbidium* have been recommended. Although some are terrestrial, they are for practical purposes treated as semi-epiphytic plants, so the tendency is to use traditional composts made up in either of the following ways:

- pine bark (60 per cent), fibrous peat (20 per cent), polyurethane moss (10 per cent), expanded polystyrene (10 per cent) and dolomite at the rate of 3 g per litre;
- medium-grained resinous bark (50 per cent), fine-grained resinous bark (40 per cent) and sand (10 per cent) and crushed oystershell (3 g per litre).

In all cases, pieces of polystyrene should be placed in the bottom of the pot for drainage. In the latter instance, the use of fine compost obviously has the effect of increasing the residual humidity of the compost.

As always, it is not merely the composition of the growing medium which is important. Rewarding cultivation of *Cymbidium*, as of other orchids, depends, in addition to the nature of the compost, on

Cymbidium
Swartz

Tribe: Cymbidieae
Subtribe: Cyrtopodiinae

Cymbidium Mimi 'Sacramento'. This is a small hybrid which has the same cultural requirements as large *Cymbidium*.

Cymbidium giganteum. This species is widely used for numerous hybridizations.

the microclimate and methods of culture employed; and it is the balance and inter-action of these three factors which makes eventual success possible.

Repotting should be carried out every two or three years, depending on the state of the compost. *Cymbidium* are grown in plastic pots of suitable size, but often these have to be quite big, given the dimensions of the plants. Pressure exerted by the roots, which tend to adhere to the sides of the pot, sometimes makes simple removal from the pot impossible. It is then best to cut the pot and delicately detach the roots from the various fragments; but in such cases the roots are often so thickly intertwined that they have to be cut through in order to divide the clumps. In some old plants, the pseudobulbs may be so tightly packed that it is extremely diffi-cult to separate them, and such drastic treatment does them no good. This is why many growers prefer not to divide the clump and to repot it in a slightly bigger container. Consequently *Cymbidium* often appear as gigantic plants which occupy a great deal of space in the greenhouse.

■ Propagation
This is done by clump division or by treat-ment of the back-bulbs.

■ Ailments

Blackened leaf tip
Possible causes are *Botrytis*, or a shortage or excess of fertilizer.

Large grey marks on the underside of leaves
Due to the presence of red spider or other mites.

Dendrobium

Swartz

Tribe: Epidendreae   Subtribe: Dendrobiinae

With more than 1400 species, the genus *Dendrobium* is one of the most diversified of the orchid family, second only to *Bulbophyllum*. Originally from South-east Asia, the *Dendrobium* have an extremely wide distribution, from the Pacific islands to the Himalayas, including Burma, Malaysia, southern China, Japan, the Philippines and Fiji.

All the *Dendrobium* are epiphytes. Because of this Olof Swartz coined the name *Dendrobium* in 1799, from the Greek *dendros* = tree and *bios* = life, in other words 'plant living on trees', a derivation almost identical to that of *Epidendrum*.

Adapted to a vast number of different habitats, *Dendrobium* vary considerably in their plant structure:

- the leaves may be flat, soft, tough, cylindrical, succulent, persistent or deciduous, long, broad, etc.;
- the pseudobulbs may be ovoid, fusiform, smooth or wrinkled, in the form of long, soft or tough canes, pendulous or erect.

Dendrobium are sympodial plants, generally with a very small rhizome from which new pseudobulbs and new roots develop every year. The flowers are very variable in form, texture and duration, but always display an identical basic structure: petals and sepals of the same size, and two lateral sepals joined to the base of the column, forming a sort of dome or chin.

These characteristics, as well as the very peculiar form of the pollinia, have made classification of this immense genus virtually impossible. Nevertheless, Bentham proposed a subdivision into seven groups, the two largest of

Dendrobium superbum. This orchid is also known as *Dendrobium anosmum* and comes from countries in South-east Asia (Laos, Vietnam and Malaysia), New Guinea and the Philippines.

plants of variable size very polymorphous plant structure	
appreciate strong lighting	
should be repotted in smallest possible containers	
repot when roots begin to grow	
simple reproduction by removing keikis, clump division or cane cuttings	
classified according to their need of water and heat into six horticultural groups; only group II *Dendrobium* can usually be cultivated indoors (see facing table)	

Dendrobium nobile. The most popular of all *Dendrobium.*

Dendrobium: the major cultural groups, as classified by Rebecca Tyson Northen				
Group	Leaves	Greenhouse	Watering	Examples
I	deciduous	intermediate, warm in summer, cool in winter	winter rest +	D. nobile, D. chrysanthum, D. wardianum
II	deciduous or coriaceous and persistent	intermediate, warm all year	winter rest +	D. speciosum, D. superbum, D. aggregatum, D. parishii, D. findlayanum, D. pierardii, D. heterocarpum
III	persistent	intermediate, warm in summer, cool in winter	no rest, simply reduce in winter	D. densiflorum, D. farmeri, D. fimbriatum, D. thyrsiflorum
IV	persistent	cool all year	short suspension early autumn	'nigro-hirsute' group: D. bellatulum Pedilonium group: D. secundum
V	persistent	intermediate	no rest or short rest after growth	D. antilope (Ceratobium group) V and VI hybrids
VI	persistent	warm	restrict twice	D. phalaenopsis, D. bigibbum, D. superbiens

Dendrobium
Swartz

Tribe: Epidendreae
Subtribe: Dendrobiinae

which are themselves subdivided into several sections:

- *Aporum* group:
  D. anceps
- *Rhizobium* group:
  D. linguiforme
- *Cadeta* group:
  D. cucumerinum
- *Strongyle* group:
  D. teretifolium
- *Sarcopodium* group:
  D. coelogyne,
  D. treacherianum
- *Stachyobium* group:
  D. speciosum,
  D. bigibbum,
  D. superbum,
  D. fytchianum,
  D. mutabile,
  D. macrophyllum,
  D. veitchianum
- *Eudendrobium* group:
  – *Pynostachya* section:
  D. secundum
  – *Formosae* section:
  D. formosum,
  D. infundibulum,
  D. draconis,
  D. lowii
  – *Calostachyae* section:
  D. chrysotoxum,
  D. brymerianum,
  D. moschatum
  – *Fasciculata* section:
  D. nobile,
  D. aureum,
  D. crassinode,
  D. wardianum

Although the subdivisions proposed by Bentham undoubtedly possess botanical and taxonomic interest, they are only of comparative value for the grower. In fact, it is either impossible or misleading to equate cultivation methods and considerations of biological and climatic conditions which the orchids enjoy in their original habitats with this classification. This is hardly surprising, given that the same section contains *Dendrobium* from China, Java, Australia and the Philippines.

More or less independently of the phylogenetic and geographic origins on which classifications are founded, *Dendrobium* are in practice adapted to all types of climate:

- cold: high-altitude *Dendrobium*, as from the foothills of the Himalayas;
- temperate: *Dendrobium* from New Zealand;
- hot and constantly humid;
- hot, with a marked dry season;
- an alternation of seasons, dry and cold, warm and humid.

The American orchid collector Rebecca Northen has therefore established a classification for *Dendrobium* which is not based on taxonomic criteria but on their combined temperature and water requirements both in nature and in the greenhouse.

The morphological features of each *Dendrobium* species may, moreover, suggest certain methods of cultivation and even help us to determine the group to which such a species might belong. Thus the colour, development and texture of the leaves can indicate the kind

Dendrobium cruentum. Originally from Burma, Thailand and the northern part of the Malaysian peninsula, it is a representative of the 'nigro-hirsute' group of *Dendrobium*.

Dendrobium Cesar × Jaq Singapor. A recently created hybrid from the 'antennatum' and 'phalaenopsis' group *Dendrobium* (below, right).

Dendrobium aureum. Also called *Dendrobium heterocarpum*, it comes from Indonesia, Southeast Asia and the Philippines.

of lighting, whether solar or artificial, that they need:

- if the leaves are soft and persistent, there is good reason to assume that the plant has no need of a rest period;
- on the other hand, leaves that are deciduous or covered by a thick cuticle which makes them coriaceous, indicate that the plant is adapted to dry conditions, which have to be reproduced in the greenhouse.

Knowing the exact origin of *Dendrobium* nevertheless remains the best possible guide.

■ Points common to all *Dendrobium*

Although they are extremely diverse, *Dendrobium*, in most essentials, have the same needs, which are outlined here.

■ Light

Almost all *Dendrobium* like strong, bright natural lighting so that they can develop healthy pseudobulbs, provided they are sheltered from intense sun which could scorch their leaves. This form of lighting is not necessary all year round, but it is an essential requirement during the active period of growth.

Because of these special lighting requirements, it is clearly difficult to grow *Dendrobium* indoors or under artificial lighting.

■ Temperature

Dendrobium can be cultivated under almost all temperature conditions; and largely because of their special requirements in terms of water and heat it has been possible to divide the genus into six cultural groups.

■ Humidity and watering

During their growth period, *Dendrobium* need to be watered abundantly, particularly in summer. Between each watering it is important to make sure that the compost dries out almost completely. Good ventilation and intermittent drying of the roots are absolute essentials; if not, the plant's respiratory function, for which the roots are mainly responsible, would be seriously compromised.

In summer a satisfactory frequency of

Dendrobium
Swartz

Tribe: Epidendreae
Subtribe: Dendrobiinae

Dendrobium Sue Samput ×
Srisom Boom. A hybrid that
belongs to the '*phalaenopsis*'
Dendrobium.

Dendrobium bigibbum. A species
originally from northern
Australia and New Guinea
which is much used for
hybridization because of its
horticultural qualities (*below*).

watering is once every two or three days.
In autumn and winter, there are two
situations to be considered:

- *Dendrobium* with persistent leaves
  should only be given the amount of
  water necessary to prevent the pseudobulbs wrinkling. i.e. a weekly watering;
- *Dendrobium* with deciduous leaves
  should be hardly watered at all, or only
  very sparingly, so as to avoid them
  drying out too much.

The optimal humidity level should be
60–70 per cent during growth; this can be
greatly reduced in the rest period.

■ Feeding
Dendrobium need plenty of fertilizer and
should be fed at least twice a month in
summer and while they are growing. Since
they are usually potted in a compost of
pine bark, they are best given a nitrogen-
rich fertilizer of the 30-10-10 type, diluted
and applied in the manner previously
indicated.

Never forget that the compost must be
thoroughly rinsed before a feed is applied
and that no fertilizer should be given
during the rest period.

■ Repotting and compost
Repotting is by far the most important
aspect of *Dendrobium* cultivation. The
plants must be given pots that are in perfect proportion to the dimensions of their
roots, i.e. as small as possible. A small pot
guarantees better drainage and a relative
drying out of the compost between each
application of water. Under these conditions the compost breaks up much more
slowly and repotting, always a traumatic
event for *Dendrobium*, only needs to be car-

Dendrobium aggregatum. This species has persistent but coriaceous leaves and has to be grown in hanging containers.

ried out every three or four years. As a rule this interval helps to produce vigorous roots, which would not be the case if repotting were done annually.

The combination of small pot and large stems often causes problems of balance, and it may be a good idea to attach the pot to a base or even hang it. When repotting, it may also be helpful to arrange a few large pebbles around the bottom of the pot. This has no adverse effect on the drainage properties and greatly impoves the balance of the plant.

Another stratagem is to set the small pot in which the *Dendrobium* is planted into a bigger pot, filling the empty space between with pebbles.

A hanging container is ideal for cultivating species with drooping stems and inflorescences. Moreover, this solution enables the plant to benefit from additional heat and light, provides improved drainage and promotes better growth.

Pots with openings pierced in the sides and bottom will also help to aerate the compost more effectively and dry it out more rapidly. Many growers grow their *Dendrobium* as epiphytes, cultivating them on bark of tree fern, cork-oak bark or even on a simple log, thus re-creating conditions of natural growth in the greenhouse.

The ideal moment for repotting, which is always an important decision, is when the roots begin to grow; this, as a general rule, happens some weeks after the plant shoot starts to develop, which for the majority of *Dendrobium*, is in spring. It is a grave mistake to repot during the rest period as this may even kill off the plant. In this respect, *Dendrobium* differ from most other orchid genera which can stand being repotted at more or less any time. Of course, the usual precautions have to be observed, especially:

- to refrain from watering for one or two weeks afterwards, keeping the plant in shade, where it is not too hot;
- to spray the foliage.

Dendrobium
Swartz

Tribe: Epidendreae
Subtribe: Dendrobiinae

Dendrobium Plum Tate ×
antennatum. The influence of
the latter species is evident
from the twisted form of the
lateral sepals.

The type of growing medium to be used will vary considerably according to the group concerned. Basically it should consist of pine bark, the granules being adapted to the size of the plant. The compost should not include constituents capable of retaining too much water, such as sphagnum moss, polyurethane moss, etc.

■ Simple propagation

Keikis As already mentioned, these are the young plantlets that sometimes develop from old shoots on the pseudobulbs. If they are carefully detached when the roots are 2–4 in (5–10 cm) long, the keikis can be repotted; they then produce plants in every way identical to the mother plants. It is an extremely easy and popular method of propagation.

Keikis are formed in spring and summer, during the period of growth. Yet their appearance in *Dendrobium* is not always a sign of successful growth. In fact, in some respects it may be seen as a survival reaction against conditions that are threatening the plant's life, one of which may be incorrect cultivation. A number of things may have gone wrong: too much nitrogen, broken shoots, damage from insects or snails, errors in watering, unsuitable temperatures, etc. Moreover, keikis often appear as a matter of course on old pseudobulbs.

It is important to note that there is a conflict between the formation of keikis and flowering. It has to be one or the other, at least on the same pseudobulb.

Clump division when repotting This is not always the best method of reproduction. If it is done with a rhizome which

Dendrobium victoriae-reginae. A species from the Philippines which grows at high altitude.

Dendrobium infundibulum. This orchid was discovered in 1858 by a missionary, C. Parish, and described in 1859 by Lindley. It comes from the montane forests of Burma and Thailand (*below*).

is very short, the shock to the plant may be too great. The modern tendency is to repot and then leave an interval of about three weeks before attempting the clump division (which is carried out on the potted plant), and not to water for a week afterwards.

As for all sympodial orchids, the rule of three should be followed, i.e. never leave the divided clumps with less than three pseudobulbs. This also has a better aesthetic effect and means that the flowers will be of better quality.

Cuttings It is possible to cut an old pseudobulb into ten or so pieces, each bearing a number of internodes. Place the portions in a warm, moist medium, simply on sand or sphagnum moss. In a few weeks some sturdy plantlets will appear and these can later be repotted.

■ Cultural groups

Taking into consideration their water and heat requirements, *Dendrobium* may be divided into six cultural groups.

Group I These are the deciduous-leaved *Dendrobium* which can be grown in the intermediate or warm house, in spring and summer, to be transferred to the cool house for the winter and kept almost without water during this period.

While they are growing, the plants should be watered and fed generously, and also given plenty of light. In winter, watering should be almost totally suspended and feeding interrupted, whilst maintaining the bright light. Should they not get this treatment during the winter, they will not begin to flower properly and the flower buds will produce only keikis.

The principal species in this group are *Dendrobium nobile*, *D. chrysanthum* and *D. wardianum*.

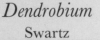

Dendrobium
Swartz

Tribe: Epidendreae
Subtribe: Dendrobiinae

Dendrobium chrysotoxum. This strongly scented species is found in southern China, the Himalayas, Burma, Thailand and Laos.

Group II These are the deciduous-leaved *Dendrobium* which have to be kept in the warm house all year round. They must be given dry conditions during the winter rest period.

Watering and feeding should be abundant in the summer. In winter, the supply of water has to be reduced to the point of just preventing desiccation, and all feeding must be suspended.

In spite of their lighting requirements, these are the only *Dendrobium* capable of adapting to life indoors because the annual and daily variations of temperature which prevail here are just about what they need.

The main species of this group are *Dendrobium anosmum, D. findlayanum, D. heterocarpum* (or *aureum*), *D. parishii, D. pierardii* and *D. aggregatum*. Note that *D. aggregatum* is included in this group although it possesses persistent (but very coriaceous) leaves.

Group III These *Dendrobium* with persistent leaves need to be cultivated, like those of group I, in the intermediate or warm house in summer and the cool house in winter. Nevertheless, by reason of their persistent leaves, they need not be so severely rationed for water. Feeding and watering must be plentiful in summer and far less frequent in winter (two or three times less), bearing in mind the minimal evaporation and the greatly diminished metabolism of the plant.

The particularly tender foliage of these species is much appreciated by red spider mite and other insect pests, so it is advisable to spray the leaves frequently with water and sometimes with insecticide or acaricide.

The principal species are *Dendrobium densiflorum, D. farmeri, D. fimbriatum, D. moschatum* and *D. thyrsiflorum*.

Dendrobium lawesii. Originally from New Guinea and the Solomon Islands, this orchid was discovered by W. G. Lawes around 1880.

Group IV Persistent-leaved *Dendrobium*, often plants from high altitude, which must be cultivated all year round in the cool house, with good lighting, but not near freezing, for the nocturnal temperature should not fall lower than 53°F (12°C) in winter and 59°F (15°C) in summer.

Watering must be suspended for a brief period of about three weeks after the growth phase, i.e. at the beginning of autumn.

Included in this group are the *Dendrobium* in the *Formosae* section, known also as 'nigro-hirsutes' (black-hairs). The principal cultivated species in this group are *Dendrobium dearei, D. formosum, D. lyonii, D. infundibulum, D. macrophyllum, D. sanderae* and *D. schwetzei*. Also included are the *Dendrobium* of the *Pedilonium* (or *Pycnostachya*) section, the best known of which are *Dendrobium secundum, D. pseudoagylome, D. ratum, D. dichaeroides, D. victoriae-reginae, D. bracteosum* and *D. smillieae*.

Group V These *Dendrobium*, likewise with persistent leaves, have requirements similar to those of group IV but are cultivated at slightly higher temperatures, i. e. in the intermediate greenhouse, with a night temperature never falling below 59°F (15°C).

There are hybrids from groups V and VI which should be grown like the *Dendrobium* of group V.

Many growers do not allow these orchids any rest period, but opinion and practice are very divided. Some growers give the plants a rest period of about three weeks after the growing period, apparently with good results.

This group includes those *Dendrobium* often known as antilope *Dendrobium* with reference to the twisted shape of their lateral petals. The principal species cultivated are *Dendrobium taurinum, D. undulatum, D. veratrifolium, D. gouldii* and *D. stratiotes*.

Group VI These are the persistent-leaved *Dendrobium* to be grown in the warm house. Night temperatures should never be lower than 59°F (15°C) in winter and 62°F (17°C) in summer. They appreciate bright light, although experience has shown that hybrids of *Dendrobium phalaenopsis* will also thrive in comparatively poor lighting conditions.

A reduction of watering after the growing period is necessary to the good formation of the inflorescence. Water abundantly once more when flowering begins, then cut back again until the new shoots appears. It is essential to spray the plant during these periods of water rationing.

Included in this group are *Dendrobium phalaenopsis* (often hybridized), among them the famous Pompadour, and also *Dendrobium bigibbum* and *D. superbiens*.

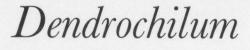

Dendrochilum
Blume

Tribe: Coelogyneae   Subtribe: Coelogyninae

In 1825 the great botanist C. L. Blume described this genus for the first time, giving it the name *Dendrochilum*, coined from the Greek words *dendros* = tree and *cheilos* = lip. The genus contains about 150 species, most of which are epiphytic (a few of them are terrestrial). The *Dendrochilum* orchids come originally from Indonesia and their distribution range covers Burma, New Guinea, Sumatra, Java, Borneo, the Philippines and all neighbouring islands.

Relatively little cultivated because of their modest flowers, these orchids nevertheless have undeniable charm; the long pendulous inflorescence has led to their being called chain orchids. Furthermore, some of them have a remarkable scent.

The epiphytic, sympodial *Dendrochilum* orchids exhibit two forms of plant structure:

- *Platyclinis* type: ovoid pseudobulbs, linked and upright, each with a persistent terminal leaf and an inflorescence developing alongside the new leaf shoot;
- *Eudendrochilum* type: separate pseudobulbs growing at intervals on a more or less branched rhizome. The inflorescence develops on a lateral flower stem.

Naturally, the second type of *Dendrochilum* has to be potted in larger containers than those used for the *Platyclinis* type.

Dendrochilum glumaceum. Originally from the Philippines, this species has small and delicately scented flowers.

modest-sized plants of 8–12 in (20–30 cm)	cultivable in intermediate house
appreciate moderate lighting	restrict watering during winter
dislike repotting, which should ideally be done every three years	simple multiplication by clump division when repotting
	reputedly easy to cultivate in greenhouse

Dendrochilum glumaceum (detail). *Dendrochilum* are also known as chain orchids.

■ Light

Denderochilum do best with moderate light; avoid direct sunlight, especially in summer.

■ Temperature

These orchids are usually grown in the warm house or in the warm part of the intermediate house. The minimal winter temperature should not be lower than 53°F (12°C).

■ Humidity and watering

Watering should be frequent and accompanied by monthly feeding during the growing stage, but reduced when the pseudobulbs are mature and the plant about to enter upon its rest period. It is not necessary, however, to suspend watering altogether.

The compost should be kept slightly moist between each watering while the plant is growing but can be allowed to dry out partially in winter.

■ Repotting and compost

Like the *Coelogyne* species, to which they are closely related, the *Dendrochilum* orchids do not like to be repotted too often. For this reason, small pots should be chosen for the operation, for they facilitate drainage and lend themselves to a compost consisting essentially of pine bark and tree fern. Sphagnum moss is nowadays used less frequently, for reasons already explained. These orchids are very sensitive to decomposition of the substrate; so they need to be repotted rapidly if warning signs of this appear.

Disa
Berg.

Subtribe: Diseae

Subtribe: Disinae

Petrus Jonas Bergius described and named the genus for the first time in 1767 in his *Discriptiones Plantarum ex Capite Bonae Spei*. According to Harry Bolus, the name may have come from the Latin *dis*, i.e. rich, in an allusion to the beauty of its flower.

Disa species were grown and hybridized with great success towards the end of the nineteenth century. After that they virtually disappeared from collections. Only quite recently did they recover the esteem, thanks mainly to South African growers who created numerous hybrids. Today there are some 200 known species, the majority from South and tropical Africa. Four species grow in Madagascar. Some of the *Disa* species certainly thrive in a warm climate but almost all the cultivated species, including the best known, *Disa uniflora*, do well in the cool house.

These are terrestrial plants which in structure greatly resemble European orchids. they have an underground tuber furnished with roots, from which a rosette of leaves and the inflorescence are formed. After flowering, one or several more tubers develop close to the old one. Moreover, suckers may appear at the base of the rosette, giving rise to young plantlets likely to flower some years later. These various structures offer many opportunities of propagating the plants in a simple manner.

Disa uniflora (side view). The loveliest orchid from South Africa's Cape Province, it is not easy to cultivate.

■ Light

Disa species must be given bright light, which is indispensable to the formation of sturdy plants and brilliantly coloured flowers. They can be grown in full sun, provided they are given some shading in the hottest part of the day.

■ Temperature

In a temperate climate, they can be cultivated without shelter out in the open, provided the temperature never falls below 32°F (0°C). A cool house, with a cooling system that furnishes excellent ventilation, and with plenty of light, provides the most favourable conditions for these orchids.

Humidity and watering

The quality of the water is of prime importance for raising *Disa* species. It should bear no traces of chlorine and as little calcium as possible. It can be slightly acid. So water treated with oxalic acid will do very well if no rain water is available.

These plants benefit from constant humidity but the compost should never be drenched. Applications of water must therefore be spaced out sufficiently to ensure correct conditions. Always water early in the morning.

Feeding

This needs to be done weekly in summer and monthly in winter, applying a balanced fertilizer in half-doses.

Repotting and compost

In their natural surroundings, *Disa* grow in aerated, well-drained soil which always retains moisture and which has an acidic pH.

Under cultivation, these conditions may be reproduced by using either of the following types of compost:

- a mixture of peat (2 parts) and perlite or vermiculite (1 part);
- pure, washed, river sand.

Disa can be repotted every year in early spring. The best container is an earthenware (unvarnished) pot, the surface evaporation of which reduces the temperature of the compost and thus the roots, which is a measure of success in cultivating the plants.

Propagation

This can be done by division, when repotting, of the rosettes and/or the tubers. Sowing, rare in the orchid world, is also possible, the *Disa* seeds being scattered on sphagnum moss or peat, which has an extraordinary success rate.

cool house plants	terrestrial plants with tuber
need for bright light	constant humidity good ventilation
apply good quality water, cool roots obtained by using earthenware pots	simple, easy propagation by division when repotting
can be propagated by sowing on peat or sphagnum	reputed to be difficult to cultivate

Disa uniflora (front view). From this angle, the extreme complexity of the flower's inner structure is evident.

Epidendrum Linné and *Encyclia* Hooker

Tribe: Epidendreae   Subtribe: Laeliinae

The *Epidendrum* species were the first orchids from tropical America to be introduced to Europe. Linnaeus initially described them in 1753 and gave the genus its name by referring to what was known of their habits (*epi* = on and *dendron* = tree). In the following years the name *Epidendrum* was applied arbitrarily to a number of other genera, originally from South America, and it was not until the works of the great nineteenth-century botanists were published that this genus was identified in a more specific manner.

Epidendrum are quite widely distributed through the entire northern part of South America and also in Central America. There are about 800 species, making them one of the largest genera in the orchid family (after *Bulbophyllum*, *Pleurothallis* and *Dendrobium*).

The genus *Encyclia*, containing plants whose flowers are sometimes not resupinate, has recently been botanically separated from the genus *Epidendrum*.

These plants vary considerably in size, appearance and structure. They are sympodial orchids, the majority of them epiphytes, with persistent leaves, either with or without pseudoebulbs.

It is as well to establish their geographical origin in order to decide the type of greenhouse to which they are best suited.

Epidendrum are reputedly easy plants to cultivate, giving an abundance of flowers. The flowering period is often very lengthy and may occur at varying times throughout the year.

■ Light

Epidendrum need fairly bright light. Some of them (e.g. *Epidendrum ibaguense*) are adapted to withstand full sun. For others, it is necessary to take the customary precautions (shade between 10.00 am and 5.00 pm in summer) to avoid exposure to direct sunlight.

■ Temperature

There are no general rules. Certain *Epidendrum* can be grown in the cool house, others in the intermediate or hot house. The

Epidendrum prismatocarpum. The species comes from Panama and Costa Rica. Its scented flowers open in late summer.

Encyclia allenoides. The *Encyclia*, closely related to the *Epidendrum*, often have a lip in the superior position. The flower is not resupinate.

decision depends on their origin. The majority are reasonably tolerant and can be raised either in the cool or intermediate greenhouse.

■ Humidity and watering

A strict watering pattern must be observed, and the procedure will depend on the plant structure:

- The absence of pseudobulbs (e.g. *Epidendrum ibaguense*) implies that the plant has no rest period. Watering should be plentiful in spring and summer, then followed by a reduced but regular rhythm in winter.
- The presence of fairly small pseudobulbs (e.g. *Epidendrum pentotis*) indicates that watering should be normal during growth and that there is a partial rest period in winter.
- The presence of strong, large pseudobulbs (e.g. *Epidendrum stamfordianum*) means that watering should be normal and abundant throughout the growing period and that there must be an absolute rest phase, without any watering, during winter (or just as much as is necessary to prevent the pseudobulbs withering).

The humidity level, high in spring and summer, needs to be lowered in winter.

■ Feeding

Apply one half-dose of 20-20-20 balanced fertilizer weekly during the active period of growth, and suspend all feeding during the winter.

■ Repotting and compost

The repotting operation is done in spring, when plant growth resumes, in a compost identical to that for *Cattleya*.

Small species may be grown on rafts of tree fern.

Repotting should be carried out in the same manner as for *Cattleya*: a plastic pot, not too big, sufficient room for the frontal bulb, suspension of watering in the months following the operation (except for occasional spraying of the leaves), and shade as required.

The plants should be repotted every other year.

■ Propagation

This may be done by clump division when repotting.

very large genus	variable size
type of greenhouse (cool, intermediate or warm) dependent on geographical origin	flowers often scented
pattern of watering according to plant structure strong pseudobulbs: absolute winter rest	flowering varies according to species, but as a rule of long duration
no pseudobulbs: no rest period	tolerant plants, easy to grow
	repot every two years in spring

Lycaste Lindley
and *Anguloa* Ruiz and Pavon

Tribe: Maxillarieae   Subtribe: Lycastinae

These two genera may be cultivated in an identical manner even though their outward appearances differ considerably. Their area of distribution is virtually the same: the whole north-western part of South America extending, in the case of *Lycaste*, into Mexico. These are orchids for the cool greenhouse, with the exception of a few *Lycaste* species which are adapted to the intermediate house.

These sympodial plants with large pseudobulbs lose their leaves, partially or completely, in autumn. The inflorescence develops at the same time as the new leaf shoot, at the base of the previous year's pseudobulb, and flowers as a rule in spring.

Anguloa

In 1794 the botanists Ruiz and Pavon described for the first time an *Anguloa uniflora*, giving it this name in tribute to Don Francisco de Angulo, director general of mines in Peru.

Anguloa and *Lycaste* are often interbred, producing hybrids with remarkable qualities known as *Angulocaste*.

There are ten or so species of *Anguloa*, the best known of which are *Anguloa ruckeri* and *A. clowesii*.

The shape of the flower, with upright sepals and petals, resembles a tulip. The loose, mobile lip is inside, facing the column which has a strange shape, like a baby in a cradle. These peculiarities explain why they are sometimes known either as tulip orchids or cradle orchids.

Lycaste

This genus was described in 1843 by Lindley who gave it this name with reference to Lycaste, daughter of Priam, King of Troy, famous for her great beauty.

There are thirty-five known species of *Lycaste*, and they fall into two categories: those that lose their leaves completely in autumn (deciduous), and those that only lose their leaves partially (semi-deciduous). Naturally, watering procedures are markedly different for these two types.

■ Light

These orchids need plenty of light, but they must never be exposed directly to the sun. Lack of light is indicated by a general wilting of the plant (poor growth or weakness of pseudobulbs and shoot).

■ Temperature

They are cultivated in the cool house (except for certain *Lycaste* species which require an intermediate house).

Both *Lycaste* and *Anguloa* orchids can occasionally tolerate extreme temperatures of 30°F (-1°C) or 91°F (33°C) without any appreciable harm. But successful flowering depends on there being a marked difference between day and night and summer and winter temperatures.

■ Humidity and watering

The surrounding humidity level should be 60 per cent during the growth phase and 40 per cent during the rest period.

Watering must be abundant while the plant is growing, greatly curtailed in autumn and almost suspended in winter, when water need only be applied to prevent the pseudobulbs withering and the compost drying out excessively. For *Lycaste* species with semi-deciduous leaves, the rest period can be somewhat less strictly observed.

The bearing of the leaves, the condition of the shoot and the appearance of the compost are all reliable indications as to when watering will be most opportune.

Finally, it is inadvisable to spray the leaves because of the undesirable marks that this may cause.

■ Feeding

Applications of a balanced fertilizer should be given twice a month for the entire period of growth.

Lycaste deppei. The species was discovered around 1828 in Mexico and grown by Loddiges (first described in 1830).

■ Repotting and compost

In nature *Lycaste* and *Anguloa* are either terrestrial or epiphytic, and some have an intermediate habit. So a number of different substrates, with varied ingredients, are likely to be used. Some growers add a little peat to make the compost heavier. One very effective mixture might consist of 40 per cent medium-grained pine bark, 30 per cent charcoal, 10 per cent perlite, 10 per cent peat and 10 per cent vermiculite.

Neither genus, as a rule, shows any resistance to being repotted. The development of the roots, often rapid, may necessitate annual repotting, especially if peat or sphagnum moss are being used. But certain species will only tolerate repotting every two years.

The best time to carry out the operation is in late winter, just before vegetative

large plants: 20–32 in (50–80 cm)	grown in cool greenhouse
must be given plenty of light	need a winter rest period with watering suspended
repot every year or every other year	reputedly easy to grow
tender deciduous leaves subject to attacks by mites in summer	cannot be grown indoors

regrowth. Either plastic pots or pierced earthenware containers will be suitable.

■ Ailments

In summer, measures must be taken against attacks by mites, which often appear on the underside of the leaves. Treat and raise the humidity level slightly.

Anguloa clowesii. Anguloa are near relatives of the *Lycaste* and because of the shape of their perianth are often called cradle or tulip orchids.

Masdevallia
Ruiz and Pavon

Tribe: Epidendreae   Subtribe: Pleurothallidinae

In 1794 Ruiz and Pavon discovered this genus in the course of an expedition to Peru. They named it in honour of the Spanish botanist Jose Masdevall. The genus has undergone a very strange succession of fortunes. Towards the end of the nineteenth century the species were very popular with collectors, but subsequently they almost vanished; only in the last ten years or so have they returned to favour.

There are more than 300 known species, with a distribution range that covers Central America and the northern part of South America.

The majority of *Masdevallia* are plants from medium and high altitudes, so they have to be cultivated in the cool greenhouse.

These orchids are often very small, their dimensions ranging from 1 to 12 in (2–30 cm). The flowers are extraordinary both for their shape and the variety and beauty of their colours. Their structure, too, is unusual. The flower itself consists essentially of three sepals, fused at the base. Petals, lip and column are sometimes reduced to a minimum, tucked away in the centre of the flower. The sepals are very often extended to form a paint; in shape, colour and direction they are extremely variable, but nonetheless very characteristic of the genus.

Unusual plants, and reasonably priced, *Masdevallia* do not have the reputation of being the easiest types of orchid to grow. It may be that this reputation has something to do with the fruitless attempts by some growers to cultivate them in other than a cool greenhouse.

Masdevallia schmidtmummii. *Masdevallia* grow mainly in the mountain forests of the Andes. The sepals are often extended in a bizarre fashion, giving the flowers a characteristic appearance.

■ Light

Contrary to some assumptions, *Masdevallia* are not true shade plants. There has been a tendency to provide them with shade in the greenhouse so as to limit a rise in temperature. But some growers do not accept that *Masdevallia* should be kept permanently in shade. Bright light which does not entail too much heat has an extremely beneficial effect on the plant, which throws out strong shoots and good quality flowers. In winter and on dark days, it is essential that blinds should be raised.

The only restriction on lighting, apart from rising temperature, will be dictated by the behaviour of the plant itself, in the event of the leaves turning pale or taking on a reddish pigmentation. Obviously, exposure to full sunlight must be avoided. There is a shade point that can be applied to the panes of the greenhouse which becomes translucent when it rains and which is, in addition, very easy to remove in autumn. This could be extremely useful in the cultivation of *Masdevallia*.

■ Temperature

Masdevallia are (with exceptions) cool house plants. The majority come originally from the mountain regions of Central America and the northern part of South America, where they are subjected to natural temperature fluctuations around 48–55°F (9–13°C) in winter and 59–64°F (15–18°C) in summer, corresponding to the normal variations found in a cool greenhouse. Sometimes, *Masdevallia* can withstand higher temperatures for brief periods; but anything above 80°F (26.5°C) is likely to prove harmful. The principal difficulty in growing them seems to be the problem of maintaining a temperature of 64°F (18°C) throughout the summer, which is virtually impossible in a small greenhouse unless equipped with an effective air-conditioning or cooling system.

Masdevallia bella (syn. *Dracula bella*). Long considered by botanists to form part of the genus *Masdevallia*, *Dracula* is now acknowledged as a distinct genus.

cool house plants (with exceptions)	impossible to grow indoors
dimensions small, even tiny	continuous growth without rest period
compost and surroundings need constant humidity and good ventilation	do not grow clumps that are too small
appreciate light but not direct sun	

Masdevallia
Ruiz
and
Pavon

Tribe: Epidendreae
Subtribe: Pleurothallidinae

Flower development depends on there being a notable difference of temperature by day and by night (at least 7–9°F/ 4–5°C). If no flower buds appear, it is possible to induce them artificially by placing the plants for a few hours in the vegetable compartment of the refrigerator, then repeating the procedure eight days later, but care must be taken over this.

■ Humidity and watering

Masdevallia live in tropical forests at an altitude where there is constant humidity. It is imperative to reproduce such conditions by giving them a high surrounding level of moisture, ventilating them sufficiently and watering them plentifully, but obviously without drenching the compost.

Since they lack a storage organ, *Masdevallia* have no rest period, so that watering need never be interrupted. Its frequency depends on the temperature, humidity and ventilation. On average, watering should take place every three or four days.

■ Feeding

This should continue all year round, once or twice a month, using a 10-10-10 type fertilizer.

■ Ventilation

Masdevallia thrive on free circulation of air. A good way to achieve this is to aerate the greenhouse with a couple of ventilators situated at ground level, which may be left open permanently in summer. In winter they can be closed at night and opened during the day. Even in midwinter it is a good idea to aerate the greenhouse, even if only briefly. Do not forget to provide the ventilators with a screen to prevent insects and rodents getting in.

Masdevallia gibberosa (syn. *Scaphosepalum gibberosum*). As its alternative names suggest, the position of this species is somewhat ambiguous. The two genera, nevertheless, are cultivated identically.

Masdevallia platiglossa. The species, from Colombia, is a uniformly pale green colour (*below, left*).

Masdevallia chimaera (syn. *Dracula chimaera*). *Dracula* may be grown in hanging baskets to allow their flowers to develop beneath the plant.

Considering the high humidity level that *Masdevallia* enjoy, the use of a ventilation system entails setting an extractor ventilator near the roof to get rid of the hottest air.

The use of an air-conditioning or cooling system is essential in all temperate and hot regions so as to solve the problem of ventilation and humidification.

■ Repotting and compost

Among the many available types of compost, orchid growers prefer those ingredients which guarantee the best possible drainage and maximum retention of moisture. One of the most popular mixtures comprises 70 per cent pine bark, 10 per cent charcoal, 10 per cent perlite and 10 per cent expanded clay. Very fine-grained constituents which could prevent adequate aeration of the roots must be avoided.

It is worth placing a few pieces of expanded polystyrene in the bottom of the pot to improve drainage, and it is important not to use charcoal pretreated for barbecues.

Repotting is generally done every two years. A longer interval might be dangerous for the plant, for the compost, which should be kept constantly moist, risks breaking up. For repotting use a plastic pot of a size suited to the dimensions of the plant. In temperate zones the best time to repot is in autumn, before the cold weather arrives, but it can be done without problems throughout the winter.

If the plant shows any signs of limpness, repot it immediately, no matter what the time of year. It may happen that a belated repotting leads to death of the roots. Formation of new roots may be induced by setting the plant in live, moist sphagnum moss, and putting it in the shade. Normal repotting should then be done when the new roots appear.

In the course of repotting, no attempt should be made to divide the clump systematically as this will adversely affect the appearance of the plant and result in flowers of poor quality. When the clump becomes too big, it loses its central leaves; the whole mass can then be divided into three or four small clumps which can be repotted and will grow without difficulty.

■ Propagation

A very simple method of multiplication is to cut a part of the rhizome which bears leaves and live roots and to repot in the normal manner.

A related genus: *Dracula*

Recently separated botanically from the genus *Masdevallia*, the species of the genus *Dracula* have inflorescences which develop downwards. They should therefore be grown in a small hanging basket with a plastic mesh so that these inflorescences can find their way out into the open after being buried for a time in the compost. All other growing conditions are as for *Masdevallia*.

Miltoniopsis
Godefroy-Lebeuf

Tribe: Cymbidieae   Subtribe: Oncidiinae

Miltoniopsis means 'resembling a *Miltonia*'. The name *Miltonia* was invented in 1837 to honour Viscount Milton, a great gardener and orchid grower; and the genus *Miltoniopsis*, applying to the so-called pansy orchids, was separated from *Miltonia* in 1976, a decision that continues to upset the traditional procedures of many growers. Nevertheless, to all intents and purposes, *Miltoniopsis* and *Miltonia* species respond to identical methods of cultivation.

These are twenty-five species of pansy orchids with a distribution range that covers Central America, the high plateaux of the Andes, western Brazil, Peru, Colombia and Bolivia.

These are sympodial plants furnished with pear-shaped pseudobulbs measuring about 4 in (10 cm), clustered closely together. The lanceolate, persistent leaves sprout from the base of the pseudobulb. Flowers last a remarkably long time (about a month) according to species. Unfortunately, the cut flowers fade very quickly.

Miltoniopsis have frequently been hybridized, and there are at present hundreds of such hybrids on the market in brilliant, velvety colours and extremely varied designs, which have only a distant relationship to botanical species. These patterns occupy the entire central part of the flower and are known as the 'mask'. In addition to interspecific hybrids, numerous hybrids have been produced by crossing *Miltoniopsis* with related genera such as *Oncidium*, *Brassia*, *Ada*, *Odontoglossum*, *Cochlioda*, etc.).

This ready capacity for hybridization is one of the characteristics of the subtribe Oncidiinae. The so-called hexageneric hybrids currently on the market contain six different genera among their ancestors. As far as can be ascertained, they would have no chance whatsoever of reproducing in nature, let alone finding a pollinating insect. Because they are adapted to the criteria of horticultural judging panels and not to the ecological interactions of the tropical forests, many of these hybrids have lost that indefinable quality, that impression of perfect harmony.

Miltoniopsis species have an extraordinary perfume which would alone justify all the hard work entailed in trying to cultivate this difficult genus.

Light

The *Miltoniopsis* orchids do not like strong light. In summer they need plenty of shade (blinds in addition to the application of shade paint).

Temperature

This is one of most delicate considerations in the cultivation of *Miltoniopsis*. The intermediate greenhouse is too warm and too bright for most of them; and the cool house is often too cold. The only solution, therefore, is to play about with different temperatures inside the greenhouse or, as Marcel Lecoufle suggests, to set up a special section where the plants will get the benefit of proper temperatures, shading, humidity and ventilation.

The most favourable temperatures fall between a minimum of 50°F (10°C) and a maximum of 68°F (20°C).

Humidity and watering

The compost used for *Miltoniopsis* must be constantly moist but never drenched.

There is no rest period. The surrounding humidity level should be high, from 70 to 80 per cent, with perfect ventilation.

Feeding

Use half-strength of 20-20-20 fertilizer every fortnight and every month in winter.

Repotting and compost

Repotting should be carried out annually, in autumn, using the smallest possible container. Plastic pots are preferable to earthenware pots.

The compost should be based on pine bark, fragments of tree fern and expanded polystyrene.

Propagation

By division of clumps while repotting. Avoid any very small clumps which are unattractive and, more important, too fragile.

Miltoniopsis Venus. This is one of the very many hybrids of pansy orchids. Most of them have a delightful perfume.

small-sized plants of 8–12 in (20–30 cm)	difficult to cultivate
shade plants	temperatures between those of the cool and intermediate greenhouse
high humidity level required	compost must be constantly moist
no rest period	good ventilation essential
repot annually in smallest possible container	propagation by clump division

Miltoniopsis masks. The singular masks of *Miltoniopsis* hybrids form delightful abstract compositions. From left to right, top to bottom: *Miltoniopsis* Blueana, *Miltoniopsis* Braise, *Miltoniopsis* Storm and *Miltoniopsis* Celle.

Odontoglossum

Humboldt, Bonpland and Kunth

Tribe: Cymbidieae   Subtribe: Oncidiinae

The first description of an *Odontoglossum* was made in 1815 by F. H. A. von Humboldt, A. Bonpland and C. S. Kunth. The idea for the name came from a characteristic of the lip which has tooth-like ridges in its centre (from the Greek *odonto* = tooth and *glossa* = tongue).

Very much the fashion at the end of the nineteenth century, *Odontoglossum* have since gone through a bad patch but for the last fifteen years have enjoyed a comeback, becoming extremely popular. It is possible that this new-found popularity has something to do with the 'modern style' with which many *Odontoglossum* flowers can be identified. There are a hundred or so species, originally from the mountain regions of Central America and the northern parts of South America.

Odontoglossum are sympodial, epiphytic plants with a flattened pseudobulb.

These plants hybridize freely with one another and also with related genera (*Miltonia, Brassia, Oncidium, Cochlioda, Osmoglossum* and *Rossioglossum*). They are all orchids for the cool greenhouse. The majority of the genera that lend themselves to such hybridization are regarded by botanists as being part of a single phylogenetic group, associated with a primitive form of *Oncidium*.

Can be grown like *Odontoglossumo*: *Osmoglossum, Rossioglossum, Cochlioda* and the majority of *Odontoglossum* hybrids with their closely related genera.

Odontioda Automate de Valec. The *Odontioda* species are hybrids of *Odontoglossum* and *Cochlioda*. This one was recently created by the firm of Vacherot et Lecoufle.

■ Light

Odontoglossum will thrive in fairly bright light provided they are not exposed directly to the sun and that their leaves do not get overheated. During winter, some growers are quite prepared to cultivate them in a greenhouse without shading or whitewash. A slight red pigmentation at the base of the leaves indicates that the plant is receiving as much light as it can stand.

In summer, the greenhouse must be shaded externally between 9.00 am and 5.00 pm, using blinds that provide 50–60 per cent shade, according to climate. As much space as possible should be left between the pane and the blind so as to prevent the greenhouse becoming too hot.

■ Temperature

Cool greenhouse conditions suit the plants best: 50–54°F (10–12°C) for the winter night temperature and 68–75°F (30–24°C) for the summer day temperature (which must not be exceeded). These are sensitive plants which can occasionally withstand levels down to 44°F (7°C) in winter but are far less capable of tolerating anything higher than 77°F (25°C) in summer.

Like all tropical plants from high altitudes, *Odontoglossum* appreciate a marked difference of day and night temperatures, e.g. 11–14°F (6–8°C).

■ Humidity and watering

Watering depends on a number of inter-related conditions, notably temperature and ventilation. In fact, a measure of skill is required to water these orchids correctly. The compost should never be allowed to dry out completely during the plant's growth phase, otherwise the

Odontoglossum schlieperianum. Found in Panama and Costa Rica, this plant, like most of the *Odontoglossum*, grows at high altitude and must be cultivated in the cool greenhouse.

cool greenhouse plants	medium to large size; 16–40 in (40–100 cm)
constant moisture required	period of winter rest
fairly strong light plus good ventilation	propagation by clump division
repot every other year in autumn or spring	water regularly during growth period
repot in small container with fine-grained compost	indoor cultivation inadvisable
Osmoglossum, Rossioglossum, Cochlioda can be grown like *Odontoglossum*	unscented flowers

Odontoglossum
Humboldt, Bonpland
and
Kunth

Tribe: Cymbidiaea
Subtribe: Oncidiinae

Odontonia Boussole 'Blanche'. A hybrid of *Odontoglossum* and *Miltonia*, this type of cross was carried out quite early in the history of orchid hybridization (1905).

Odontioda Marie-Noël. Like many *Odontoglossum* hybrids, this was an ideal subject for artists at the turn of the century (*below*).

development of the shoot will be retarded and not resumed until the next watering. Moreover, the aesthetic effect is disastrous, for the shoot will look warped or wrinkled, as will the leaves, which then become tapered almost to the point of disappearance. Constant humidity is therefore essential both for *Odontoglossum* and related genera: but obviously the plants must not be drenched, which will cause the roots to rot.

Odontoglossum have no rest period, so that watering must be continued in the winter, applications being more spaced out and determined by relative temperature and moisture conditions.

The plants do well with humidity maintained at 70–80 per cent. At this level the ventilation must be perfect so as to prevent any risk of attack by fungi and bacteria.

■ Feeding

A satisfactory feeding programme entails the use of a 20-20-20 fertilizer, almost continuously, in quarter-doses, i.e 0.25 g per litre. The procedure should be as follows:

- in the active growth period: a thorough rinse of the compost in pure water, then three feeds followed by normal watering;
- in winter: one feed, followed by three normal waterings.

■ Flowering

It sometimes happens that two or three inflorescences · grow on the same plant. Flower formation is always to the detriment of the plant's energy and food stocks. There is thus a risk that the flowers of *Odontoglossum*, which are numerous and which are of considerable size (sometimes

Odontoglossum constrictum. This orchid comes from Venezuela, Colombia and Ecuador, and was first described in 1843.

Maclellanara Pagan Lovesong. This famous American hybrid is cultivated like *Odontoglossum* (*below*).

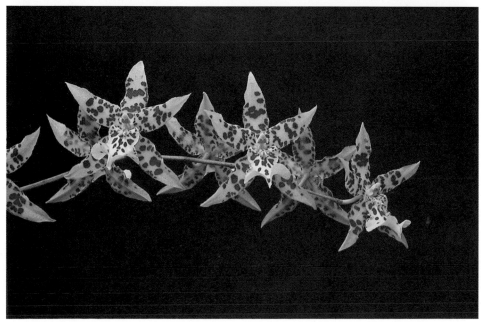

2–3 in/6–8 cm across), will exhaust the plant.

As a result, it is worth observing the following rules:

- remove inflorescences if the plant possesses only two pseudobulbs, or if they develop on a pseudobulb which is too small or too young;
- to not allow more than one inflorescence to develop on each plant.

■ Repotting and compost

Among the various composts suggested, the following are most frequently used:

- a mixture of coarse sand, peat, pine bark and perlite, all in equal quantities;
- a mixture of 50 per cent bark, 25 per cent expanded polystyrene and 25 per cent polyurethane moss; to this mixture a little dolomite lime may be added.

All the different ingredients should be fine-grained.

It is worth mentioning, incidentally, that perlite dust may be extremely irritating to the lungs if inhaled by accident.

Repotting should be done every two years, the best time being just after flowering, i.e. in autumn. Use the smallest possible pot because these plants react badly to being repotted in a container that is too large. To prevent any risk of rotting, suspend all watering except for spraying the foliage. Provide temporary shade, as usual, for newly repotted plants.

■ Propagation

This may be done in one of two ways:

- By dividing the clump in the course of repotting, observing the so-called rule of three. When carrying out this operation, examine the cut rhizome very carefully to make sure there is no sign of fungal or bacterial infection. If there is, cut the rhizome again until you have an unaffected portion. The knife must be sterilized for each cut to prevent any chance of germs being tranferred to healthy tissues.
- By treating the back-bulbs, providing three of such bulbs are kept together after making certain they are clean.

Oncidium
Swartz

Tribe: Cymbidieae

Subtribe: Oncidiinae

The genus was given this name in 1800 by Olof Swartz because of the small tubercles situated at the base of the lip which bear a resemblance to tumours (Greek *onkos*). *Oncidium* is, after *Dendrobium* and *Bulbophyllum*, one of the biggest genera, containing more than 750 species; their range covers the whole of central and tropical America, from Florida to southern Argentina. But the largest number of species come from Brazil and the Colombian Andes, Ecuador and Peru.

Despite this vast area of distribution and immense diversity of species and habitats (from sea level to an altitude of 13,000 ft/4000 m), the majority of *Oncidium* are tolerant plants, adaptable to a wide variety of cultivation techniques. Given the minimum attention and with observation of a few basic rules, it is quite easy to obtain superb flower spikes, branched or unbranched, erect, curving or pendulous. The dimensions of the plants range from a few centimetres to more than a metre, and in the case of *Oncidium orgyale* or *O. macranthum*, to 17–20 ft (5–6 m). The number of flowers is also highly variable: thus *O. kramerianum* and *O. papilio* each bear only one or two flowers at any one time, whereas *O. harrisonianum* produces hundreds.

Yellow and brown are the most common colours but in fact these orchids exhibit the entire range from green to purple, mauve and vermilion, not to mention white.

Oncidium forbesii. Discovered by George Gardner in 1837 in eastern Brazil, it was named after H. O. Forbes, gardener to the Duke of Bedford.

■ Light

Oncidium must be given plenty of light. Although the green parts of the plant develop quite well in relatively weak light, flower growth will be inhibited or even prevented. A slight variation in the amount of light provided will often be enough to achieve a compromise, balancing the growth and flowering factors.

■ Humidity and watering

Oncidium thrive on a rapid alternation of wet and dry conditions. In this sense they stand midway between *Miltonia*, which need a compost that is constantly moist, and *Cattleya*, which only need watering at weekly intervals. So the watering cycles vary quite considerably, depending on species, from one to three days: every day for the so-called equitants, where the compost takes only half a day to dry, and three-day intervals for the round-leaved *Oncidium* which do best with longer dry phases.

■ Feeding

Applying fertilizer is obviously pointless during the rest period. *Oncidium* benefit greatly from a weekly or fortnightly feed while they are growing. Here again there is a natural conflict between plant growth and flower development. Applications of fertilizer in the recommended doses will stimulate the green parts but inhibit the flowers; so some growers either cut down the dosage or simply reduce the amount of nitrogen during this period.

■ Ventilation

Oncidium do best with plenty of air, not too moist (60 per cent humidity) and constantly in movement: a light, cool breeze, in fact, which quickly dries out their roots.

Marks on the flowers and rotting of the leaves are the customary warning signs of excess humidity.

plants of very variable size and structure	always need very strong light
all may be cultivated in the intermediate greenhouse	frequent watering with alternating damp and dry phases
small species may be grown on tree fern rafts	repot every other year (except group IV)

Oncidium: cultural groups (after Lee C. Soule)				
Groups	**Characteristics or names**	**Light**	**Watering**	**Examples**
Group I	*Oncidium* with mottled leaves	Good, but not too strong light	No rest period	*O. papilio, O. kramerianum*
Group II	*Oncidium* with tender pseudobulbs	Average light	No rest period	*O. sphacelatum, O. meirax, O. varicosum, O. tetracopax, O. uniflorum, O. ornithorhynchum, O. macranthum*
Group III *Oncidiums* without pseudobulbs or with atrophied pseudobulbs	Mule-eared *Oncidium*	Average light	Restrict severely after flowering	*O. luridum, O. uniflorum, O. cavendishianum O. carthagenense, O. stramineum, O. lanceanum*
	Equitant *Oncidium*	Average light	Restrict severely after flowering	*O. calochilum, O. caribense, O. tetrapetalum, O. urophyllum, O. compressicaule, O. pulchellum, O. triquetrum, O. guianense*
	Oncidium with cylindrical leaves: rat tails	Strong light	Absolute rest (one month at least after flowering)	*O. jonesianum, O. stipitatum, ·O. splendidum, O. cebolleta, O. sprucei*
Group IV	*Oncidium* with hard, round pseudobulbs	Maximum light	No rest period. Essential to dry out between waterings	*O. cheirophorum, O. onustum, O. ampliatum, O. tigrinum, O. globuliferum, O. bifolium, O. maculatum*

Oncidium
Swartz

Tribe: Cymbidieae
Subtribe: Oncidiinae

Repotting and compost

As a general rule, earthenware pots are preferable to ordinary plastic pots because the compost dries out more quickly in them and the roots remain cooler, particularly in summer; but perforated plastic pots are also satisfactory. All containers should be sufficiently small to allow the roots to dry out, but not too small to prevent proper development of the plant. For the same reason, it is important to leave enough room in front of the most recent shoot.

Repotting should be carried out every other year, except for plants of group IV (see p. 165), for in their case the structure of the compost, being less frequently watered, does not change so rapidly. The orchids in this group, therefore, only need repotting every three or four years.

Almost all of the *Oncidium* will grow quite happily in well-drained compost based on pine bark or osmunda fibre; and cultivation on logs or bark provides them with growing conditions as nearly as possible equivalent to those the plant finds in nature.

Culture of the four *Oncidium* groups

Although most authors persist in classifying *Oncidium* according to the prevailing temperatures in their original habitats, it makes better sense to group them in relation to their physical appearance. In most cases, *Oncidium* are sufficiently tolerant to be cultivated in the intermediate house. In fact, provided all other growing conditions are respected, it would seem that they are not too particular about temper-

ature. On this basis, therefore, we can divide *Oncidium* into four groups, taking account not only of the horticultural features but also the relationships of the species concerned; for phylogenetic affinities determine the possibilities of hybridization within each of these groups.

Group I

These *Oncidium* with mottled leaves are divided into six species, the best known of which are *Oncidium papilio* and *O. kramerianum*. Their attribution to the genus *Oncidium* is contested by some taxonomists (mainly because of the number of chromosomes they possess). The main feature of this group is the absence of any rest period.

Light

These plants require abundant, but not too bright, light because they cannot stand full sun. Broadly speaking, therefore, they do well in the same lighting conditions that are applicable to *Phalaenopsis*,

Oncidium sarcodes. This species is so named because of the fleshy appearance of its petals.

Odontocidium Selsfield Gold. Crosses of *Odontoglossum* and certain species of *Oncidium* have produced some remarkable hybrid (*below*, *right*).

Oncidium Golden Sunset. This is a superb and aptly named hybrid of the equitant oncidiums.

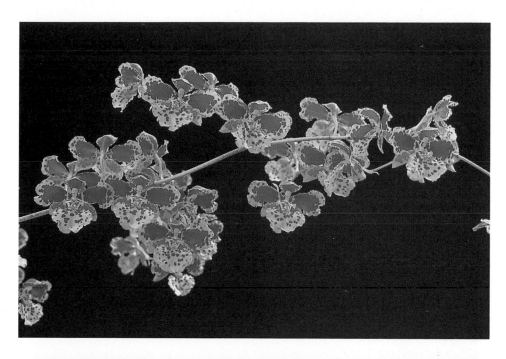

alongside which they may be cultivated. The sign they are getting too much light is slight wasting of the leaf shoots and a deep red pigmentation which may even affect the underside of the leaves. The leaves may subsequently turn a sickly yellow and lose their mottled appearance.

Humidity and watering
Patterns of watering are very variable and dependent on several factors, notably temperature, surrounding humidity and ventilation. The aim is to keep the roots constantly damp, in a moist environment which, whilst perfectly drained, must never be soaked.

Compost
Osmunda is certainly one of the best ingredients for satisfying these criteria. Conifer bark is equally effective.

Flowering
Oncidium kramerianum and *O. papilio* flower at different times and often for several successive months on the same inflorescence, which develops from the base of the pseudobulbs. Naturally, this spike should not be cut when a flower fades, since one flower follows another.

    Oncidium limminghei, which belongs to the same group, only produces one or two flowers, without blooming again on the same spike.

Cultural note
Roots that are in poor condition or light that is too strong will both lead to the same outcome: falling leaves. The most effective remedy to consider, apart from eventually changing the compost and adjusting the lighting and rhythm of watering, is to place the plant in that part of the greenhouse where *Phalaenopsis* species are seen to be doing best.

■ Group II
These *Oncidium* are described as having tender pseudobulbs. Although the plants themselves are not truly tender, in shape and texture they bear a resemblance to *Odontoglossum* and *Miltonia*, being closely related, both morphologically and physiologically, to these two genera. The pseudobulbs are large and often pear-shaped, with leaves and bracts at the base and one or two leaves at the tip. The plants do well in the cool house, with little light.

    The principal species are: *Oncidium*

Oncidium
Swartz

Tribe: Cymbidieae
Subtribe: Oncidiinae

sphacelatum, O. uniflorum, O. meirax, O. spilopterum, O. ornithorhynchum and *O. varicosum*.

Light

The orchids of this group like average lighting conditions (60–70 per cent). The amount of light is crucial, for if it is too low, the plant wilts. At 55 per cent and above, the green parts develop well, but 60–65 per cent is about right for high quality flowering (number of flowers, perfect form and colour, and maximum duration). Anything above 70 per cent cannot be tolerated by these plants.

Humidity and watering

These *Oncidium* observe no rest period, so they grow almost continuously. Thus they have to be watered regularly all year round. The appearance of the pseudobulbs gives a useful indication of the plant's water content; if too low, the pseudobulbs wrinkle and then develop ridges; this symptom must not be confused with the normally wrinkled aspect of older pseudobulbs.

■ Group III

These are known as *Oncidium* without pseudobulbs. In fact, the pseudobulbs are, generally speaking, very small and virtually concealed close to the rhizome. This group is divided into three subgroups:

● The mule-eared *Oncidium*, so called after the shape and texture of their leaves: *Oncidium luridum, O. cavendishianum, O. carthagenense, O. stramineum, O. aurisasinorum*, etc.

● The equitant *Oncidium*, so called because of their overlapping leaves which spread out like a fan: *Oncidium calochilum, O. compressicaule, O. caribense,*

Oncidium cebolleta. An *Oncidium* with one of the widest ranges of distribution, comprising almost the whole of intertropical America.

Oncidium harrisonianum. William Harrison discovered this Brazilian orchid in 1831. The flower spikes of some *Oncidium* are so densely packed that they resemble a swarm of bees (*below*, *left*).

O. pulchellum, O. tetrapetalum, O. triquetrum, O. urophyllum, O. variegatum, O. guiananense, etc.

- The rat-tail *Oncidium* with cylindrical leaves: *Oncidium jonesianum, O. cebolleta, O. stipitatum, O. sprucei, O. splendidum, O. stacyii.*

Light
This third group needs plenty of light. The following precautions, however, should be observed:

- never expose the plant too suddenly to full sunlight;
- allow for a transitional period when the plant can adapt gradually to progressively brighter light; otherwise there is a risk that the often very thin leaves of these equitants may scorch;
- red pigmentation of the foliage is a sign that the plant is receiving too much light; reduce the lighting a bit in order to encourage satisfactory growth and flowering. During the months of rest that follow flowering, these *Oncidium* need a maximum amount of light (90–100 per cent). In the period of plant growth and in the course of flowering, lighting should be markedly reduced (75–80 per cent).

Attention to these changing light levels is designed to reproduce the physiological conditions enjoyed by these plants in their natural habitat; wet periods of vegetative growth when they benefit from the slight shade provided by the upper branches, a rest period, and also a dry period when the branches lose their leaves partially or completely.

Humidity and watering
A considerable reduction in watering is likewise necessary for these plants in order to reproduce the physiological rest phase which in their original habitat corresponds to the dry season. Watering must be almost totally suspended for about one month, but without letting the equitants dry out too much. If that happens, they are likely to lose their leaves.

During the growth stage, watering should be regular but somewhat less frequent than for the species of group II.

In this context, there are two essentials to note:

- take care never to let water stagnate at the base of the leaves (which may frequently happen because of their overlapping structure) as this may cause them to rot;
- be careful about watering in overcast weather, if necessary turning the plant over and shaking it gently after applying water; do this in the morning so that the plant benefits from daytime evaporation.

■ Group IV
This group comprises the *Oncidium* with hard, round pseudobulbs which wrinkle rapidly with age. It includes *Oncidium cheirophorum, O. globuliferum, O. onustum, O. bifolium, O. ampliatum, O. maculatum* and *O. tigrinum.*

The needs of these orchids are simple: maximum light, no rest period and regular watering (every two or three days), allowing the compost to dry out between each application.

Oncidium howeara. This is one of the 750 species of *Oncidium,* part of the group of equitants, but rarely cultivated.

Paphiopedilum

Pfitz.

Subfamily: Cypripedioideae

The Cypripedioideae, better known as lady's slipper orchids, derive their name from the very individual shape of their lip, which forms a pocket (or slipper) in front of the flower. *Cypripedium* itself originates in two Greek words, *Cypros* = Cyprus (the isle sacred to Venus) and *pédilon* = slipper. This feature is a virtual trap into which a pollinating insect falls; it can only escape by one of two exits, at the rear, where the pollinia stick to its back. Pollination is effected later when the same insect, imprisoned in another flower, attempts to break free: the pollinia stuck to its back are then deposited on the stigma (situated just in front of the pollinia), this being accomplished by a very subtle hook system. This, of course, is only one of the many extraordinary strategies whereby orchids are fertilized.

Botanists recognize four different genera of Cypripedioideae, all or almost all terrestrial:

- *Cypripedium*, from temperate zones of the northern hemisphere;
- *Phragmipedium*, from South America;
- *Selenipedium*, from South America;
- *Paphiopedilum*, from the Far East.

These three last genera may be cultivated in almost identical ways.

For many botanists, the Cypripedioideae are not, strictly speaking, orchids, but belong to a separate family, certainly related, but nonetheless distinct. This claim is founded on the very special structure of the column and, above all, on the presence of two lateral stamens and two stigmas, whereas other orchids have only one central stamen and one stigmatic cavity. On the basis of this argument, these authors maintain that the Cypripedioideae should be considered an earlier, side or archaic branch of the order Orchidales; a form which would thus be very ancient and primitive, despite the complexity of its flower structure and its physiology.

The genus *Paphiopedilum* was for a long time known incorrectly as *Cypripedium* in horticultural circles, and this confusion still exists. There are about sixty species distributed over the whole of South-east Asia, from the high hills of northern India to the lowlands of the Philippines.

The majority of *Paphiopedilum* are plants that grow in relative shade and in the humus of the undergrowth. Unlike orchids from temperate zones, they do not require any particular type of compost. The only condition is that this compost should be well drained and that it should contain adequate organic material. In this they are very similar to epiphytic orchids and it is for this reason that certain rare species, such as *Paphiopedilum lowii*, grow as epiphytic plants and even, in the case of *P. niveum*, as lithophytes (growing on rocks).

The *Paphiopedilum*, moreover, lack storage organs, for they are acaulous plants, without stems. Thus the inflorescence, which bears the flowers, must not be mistaken for a stem. As a rule the plants produce only a single flower, although certain species display several flowers (2–12) at a time. The few sheath-like leaves are persistent and their bases overlap one another.

Time of flowering varies a good deal but as a rule is between autumn and spring. Many hybrids flower in a completely unpredictable manner, sometimes two or three times a year, and this is undeniably an advantage to growers, for such variability among different species enables them to have flowers at various stages virtually throughout the year. Besides, these may last 6–8 weeks or even longer.

The slightly waxy texture of the flower parts accounts for this extended duration, which is quite common in the world of orchids. After all, the pollination processes are so uncertain, the longer the flowering period, the greater the chances of pollination. The cut flowers also last for a remarkable length of time, about three weeks and sometimes more, provided they are gathered eight days or so after they open.

For all these reasons, *Paphiopedilum* are extremely popular, constituting one of the five or six genera most frequently encountered in horticulture. Furthermore, they have given rise to a vast number of hybrids ever since such

average to large plants: 16–32 in (40–80 cm)	can be grown in the intermediate greenhouse
cool period necessary to induce flowering	undemanding as regards light
water regularly throughout year, with no rest period	compost must be constantly damp but not saturated
good ventilation essential	repot annually or every 2–3 years, in the smallest possible pot
easy to cultivate in greenhouse	may be grown indoors with suitable equipment

experiments began. In the nineteenth century, collectors paid exorbitant sums of money to acquire these orchids. Today, however, despite their rediscovery, they no longer arouse the same measure of excitement and are for the most part modestly priced. One exception to this rule is the celebrated *Paphiopedilum rothschildianum*, undoubtedly one of the most spectacular species, but also one of the most temperamental: it grows extremely slowly and, because of this, is very expensive.

Paphiopedilum are easy to cultivate and, provided standard precautions are taken, can even be grown indoors. However, getting them to reflower every year and keeping them alive and healthy for, say, ten years, is a skilled and fairly difficult process, and only the basic principles can be indicated here.

Paphiopedilum fairrieanum Stein. An Indian species from Assam, Sikkim and Bhutan which grows at an altitude of 4200–10,000 ft (1300–3000 m)

Paphiopedilum
Pfitz.

Subfamily: Cypripedioideae

■ Light

Growing at ground level in the dense tropical forests, *Pathiopedilum* can get by with very little light. This characteristic makes them very useful house plants, provided they are given satisfactory temperature and humidity levels.

Under natural conditions, then, *Paphiopedilum* often lack light. But in cultivation they only give of their best if they are provided with moderate yet sufficient light. So they have to be given average lighting, not too bright and obviously not direct sunlight, which would irremediably scorch their leaves. Indoors, fluorescent lighting, of the type used in conjunction with trolley cultivation (see page 38), is highly recommended.

Young plants, as well as weak ones, need less light than strong, adult specimens. It is not always easy to decide on a satisfactory compromise, but the following signs will help to strike a balance:

- too much light causes the leaves to turn yellow or sometimes to take on a suspiciously pale green tone;
- too little light may result in the leaves turning dark and, above all, in the failure of the plant to flower.

■ Temperature

Paphiopedilum may be broadly divided into two groups:

- those with uniformly green leaves which need fairly cool temperatures;
- those with mottled leaves which prefer fairly warm conditions.

Ideally, although there are exceptions, the green-leaved species should be cultivated with *Cymbidium* and the mottled-

Paphiopedilum Delrosi. In this famous hybrid obtained in 1954, the influence of *Paphiopedilum rothschildianum* is clearly discernible.

Paphiopedilum tonsum Stein. Discovered by Charles Curtis in Sumatra around 1880, its distribution range extends to northern Borneo (*below*, *left*).

Paphiopedilum rothschildianum. Originally from north-east Borneo, this is the most renowned and spectacular of all the *Paphiopedilum*. Because of its slow growth it is a rare and much valued plant.

leaved species with *Cattleya*. Nevertheless, where temperature is concerned, *Paphiopedilum* exhibit a wide tolerance range. Many growers, amateur and professional alike, raise both categories quite successfully in the intermediate greenhouse, making sure, however, that those with uniformly green leaves are grown in the cooler part and the others in the warmer part.

Hybrids furthermore, are inclined to be even more adaptable and less dependent on rigidly defined temperature patterns.

As a broad guide, no matter what the species, the average recommended temperatures are as follows:

	Night	**Day**
Paphiopedilum with uniformly green leaves	50–55°F) (10–13°C)	70–80°F) (21–27°C)
Paphiopedilum with mottled leaves	61–66°F) (16–19°C)	70–80°F) (21–27°C)

Annual variations of temperature can safely be maintained within these extremes, except for a particular period of 2–8 weeks when the night temperature needs to be quite low (50–57°F/10–14°C), so as to induce the flower buds. In temperate parts of the northern hemisphere this is easily done in September–October. Such conditions can be met by placing the plant outdoors, by keeping it for a while in the cool house or by playing around with the temperatures inside the intermediate house.

Once this induction period is over, and as soon as flower growth appears to be as satisfactory as that of the leaves, it is safe to return to normal night temperatures. It is possible – and many growers have tried it – to produce a second flowering period by lowering the temperature towards the end of spring; this should produce flowers in early autumn.

Paphiopedilum
Pfitz.

Subfamily: Cypripedioideae

Paphiopedilum hirsutissimum. The species comes from the Himalayas, from Assam and the Khasia hills. Lindley gave it this name because of the very hairy outer surfaces of the sepals, the ovary and the bract.

Paphiopedilum sukhakulii. Very close to *Paphiopedilum wardii*, it was given individual identity in 1965. Its range is extremely restricted (certain zones of north-east Thailand) (*below*).

There are, however, certain special cases:

- some mottled-leaved species, such as *Paphiopedilum venustum*, prefer the cool greenhouse;
- too much heat, above 80°F (27°C) is harmful to *Paphiopedilum* but will not kill them provided it is only a temporary situation; in this event, care must be taken to spray water on the leaves and to make absolutely certain that these are dry at nightfall;
- certain *Paphiopedilum*, such as *Paphiopedilum* Maudiae do not need low temperatures in order to induce flowering;
- very young plants develop much better with rather higher night temperatures (64–68°F/18–20°C). Indeed, this applies to all orchids;
- some species, like *Paphiopedilum fairrieanum*, have buds that will grow, very slowly, at temperatures of 50–55°F (10–13°C);
- certain growers systematically lower the greenhouse night temperature for *Paphiopedilum* to 50°F (10°C) during the entire winter, without any apparent adverse effect.

■ Humidity and watering
Paphiopedilum are semi-terrestrial plants, without storage organs, and must therefore be watered regularly all year round, without a rest period. The frequency will vary, of course, according to season and temperature; weekly in winter and more frequently (two or three times a week) in summer.

The secret of successful watering is to ensure that the compost is always damp; but if it is done too often, the compost will be saturated and the roots will inevitably

Phragmipedium Schroderae. The genus is related to *Paphiopedilum* and the constituent species are likewise known as slipper orchids; but they are distinguished mainly by the texture and form of their lateral petals.

rot. On the other hand, if the intervals between watering are too great, the compost will dry out, with equally catastrophic results: bark, which is the usual compost ingredient for *Paphiopedilum*, seldom re-absorbs water after being dehydrated and thus the hydric balance of the compost is completely upset. The only solution in this case is to soak the pot for a couple of hours after dehydration occurs, although this should only be an occasional last resort.

Watering *Paphiopedilum* therefore requires a good deal of dexterity and intuition, and is virtually an art. There is an old French saying which may be paraphrased as follows: 'If a *Cymbidium* looks thirsty, water it. If a *Cattleya* or a *Phalaenopsis* looks thirsty, wait a day or two. If a *Paphiopedilum* looks thirsty, you should have watered it yesterday.' This implies that the telltale signs of thirst are largely matters of observation, intuition and experience.

As a general rule, it is worth bearing in mind that the warmer it is, the more the plants need water and humidity. Always do the watering in the morning and, when spraying, make sure the water does not collect in the sheath of the leaves, which must be absolutely dry by evening to avoid the risk of rotting. Spraying at intervals ensures that the plant will not suffer in the event of a sudden rise in temperature. A humidity level of around 60–70 per cent is recommended in summer, and of about 40–50 per cent in winter.

■ Feeding

Over-feeding may have drastic consequences, as is the case for all orchids but particularly for *Paphiopedilum*. The frequency and type of feeding depends much on the nature of the compost and its organic content:

- If the compost contains fern roots, it is, in the opinion of some authors, practically useless to feed it; but because the composts mostly used nowadays are deficient in organic materials, feeding becomes necessary. It should be carried out once a month in winter and two or three times a month in summer.
- If the compost contains bark, give it a nitrogen-rich (30-10-10) feed.
- If it is completely devoid of organic materials, go for the 10-10-10 formula.

This last formula may be modified according to the season, adding or interspersing a

Paphiopedilum
Pfitz.

Subfamily: Cypripedioideae

Paphiopedilum glaucophyllum. In 1900 the Belgian botanist J. J. Smith described this species from Java.

Paphiopedilum Frau Ida Brandt. A very old hybrid in which the influence of *Paphiopedilum curtisii* is noticeable.

Paphiopedilum primulinum. From Sumatra, the species was first described in 1973 (*below, right*).

fertilizer with a higher phosphate content when the flowers are forming and with more nitrogen during the growth period.

A useful technique is to alternate applications of water and fertilizer. Never forget, however, to rinse the compost with fresh water before giving it a feed.

■ Ventilation

Good air circulation is important for keeping the leaves cool and for drying them sufficiently quickly to prevent any bacterial or fungal attack, particularly the dreaded bacterium *Erwinia cypripedii* which is responsible for leaf rot.

Obviously, air that is too dry is to be avoided.

■ Repotting and compost

Repotting needs to be done in spring before the compost (and in the case of *Phaphiopedilum*, this is essentially the pine bark which is so often the main ingredient) begins to break up. Signs of decomposition are likely to appear within anything from eighteen months to three years; if a longer time is allowed to elapse, problems may occur:

- excess water retention can cause the compost to be permanently saturated, so that the roots, as they gradually become detached from the slivers of bark, are likely to rot;
- later on, the bark debris is gradually washed away, water is no longer retained and the plants die of thirst, no matter what method of watering is adopted.

Because of this risk, repotting should proceed without delay, using a pot which is not too big, but just about the right size, in proportion to the roots and leaves. This will permit the roots to penetrate every

part of the compost and attach themselves properly, as they are inclined to do, to the inner surface of the pot.

Certain types of compost contain soluble salts, which do not serve any useful purpose since they are washed away as soon as the plants are watered. The following mixture is the one most frequently employed, and it has the merit of giving good results: 85 per cent pine bark, size from 2 mm to 5 mm depending on the size of the plant, 10 per cent charcoal and 5 per cent expanded polystyrene, with the addition of dolomite lime or crushed marble.

From time to time it is worth checking the pH of the compost in the following manner: take an equal volume of water and compost, let it soak overnight, then filter the water and measure the pH with indicator paper. If the pH, which should be between 7 and 6.5, is lower than 6.5, the pot should be sprinkled with a small quantity of dolomite lime.

■ Propagation

Clump division of *Paphiopedilum* plants is a very controversial subject, but can be attempted, always bearing in mind the following points:

- in order for a plant to be healthy, it must have at least three shoots;
- a clump must be well furnished to look attractive;
- there is no obligation to divide the clump every time it is repotted;
- the bigger the plant, the better the flowers;
- the best time to divide clumps is in early summer;
- do not water newly repotted plants; merely spray them until the new roots appear;
- avoid high temperatures and shade the plants; avoid cold nights.

All these precautions will help to accelerate scar formation over wounds caused by repotting.

Phalaenopsis
Blume

Tribe: Vandeae   Subtribe: Sarcanthinae

Originally established in 1825 by C. L. Blume, this genus has been modified several times, notably by H. G. Reichenbach in 1862, R. A. Rolfe in 1886 and H. Sweet in 1968. Such alterations were justified by the discovery of new species and the need to regroup these species into different sections. Named after their resemblance to moths (from Greek *phalaina* = moth and *opsis* = likeness), *Phalaenopsis* is today represented by forty-six species, many of which are ignored by orchid collectors. Their distribution covers India, Southeast Asia, the Philippines and northern Australia.

These are epiphytes, sometimes lithophytes, which grow principally in the dense, wet forests of regions where there is a marked contrast of day and night temperature (71°F/22°C by night, 95°F/35°C by day). They are usually to be found at altitudes of between 650 and 1300 ft (200 and 400 m).

The genus has been widely used by growers for intrageneric and intergeneric hybridization, with a view to obtaining plants that are often far removed from their botanical species relatives, but which possess characteristics that best conform to different horticultural criteria, namely: general form of flower (the modern trend being to have these as rounded as possible), homogeneity of colour (pure white, purple, yellow, pink, striped, etc.), texture, number of flowers, duration of flowering, habit of inflorescence, etc.

More than 5000 hybrids have so far been listed in the Sander's List of Orchid Hybrids, now published jointly by the RHS (London) and the AOS (USA). Very often their genealogy goes back ten generations or more and for that reason is extremely complex. The difficulty in establishing this with any accuracy is often compounded by the fact that classifications have been altered since the early part of the present century and that growers have sometimes been imprecise in their descriptions of parentage.

As a general rule, *Phalaenopsis* hybrids are easier to cultivate than the species, inasmuch as they are no longer dependent, as are their botanical ancestors, upon a particular culture regime, due to the countless intervening crosses which have completely upset their original genetic heritage.

Phalaenopsis lindenii. Named in honour of Lindley, the species has been widely hybridized, particularly with *Phalaenopsis equestris*.

These plants have been hybridized with a number of related genera, including *Doritis* (to produce large numbers of purple flowers), *Vanda*, *Rhynchostylis*, *Arachnis*, *Renanthera*, *Aerides* and several others. Such hybrids, for the most part, tolerate varied conditions and adapt well to an indoor climate. Some of them, in fact, can hardly be bettered as house plants, flowering for a long time, each flower staying open for several days or even weeks before being replaced by another. So it is not uncommon for a plant to continue flowering for several months.

warm house plants	adult plants very tolerant
excellent house plants	water regularly, with no rest period and no total drying out between applications
moderate shading	
avoid water stagnating in leaf sheaths	lower temperature in autumn to obtain an inflorescence
propagate by taking keikis	repot on average every other year in summer or spring

Phalaenopsis amabilis. This orchid was described in 1753 by Linnaeus in his *Species Plantarum* under the name *Epidendrum amabile.* C. L. Blume included it in the genus *Phalaenopsis* which he created in 1825. The flowers, with their purity, airy elegance and complex structure, are well nigh perfect.

■ Light

These are plants which like moderate lighting. Indoors, as in the greenhouse, a few simple, but imperative, rules need to be observed:

- never, except in winter, expose *Phalaenopsis* to full sun, which scorches their leaves;
- if grown indoors, put them in an east-facing position, with the light screened by net curtains;
- in temperate zones, shade them in summer between 11.00 am and 5.00 pm;
- in the tropics, *Phalaenopsis* should be grown under shading (about 60 per cent shade).

■ Temperature

Adult plants adapt well to a house temperature of 64–68°F (18–20°C). Such levels are somewhat removed from their original climate where the temperature seldom falls below 75–77°F (24–25°C). In fact, *Phalaenopsis* grow best at 77–86°F (25–30°C), provided they are given a high level of humidity. Obviously these are the conditions that growers endeavour to obtain in the greenhouse and they are indispensable to the normal growth of young plants.

Phalaenopsis
Blume

Tribe: Vandeae
Subtribe: Sarcanthinae

Phalaenopsis Ebauche. A contemporary hybrid with flowers of singular appearance.

Once adult, the majority of *Phalaenopsis* tolerate much lower temperatures, as will be found in a house or flat. Nevertheless, it is worth noting that the zones of tolerance here are fairly limited, for only a slight drop in nocturnal temperature (below 59°F/15°C), will destroy the flower buds, which wither, turn yellow and drop off. This is a not inconsiderable risk given that many species flower in February.

If variations in day and night temperatures are important, so too are the seasonal variations. Thus it is essential to be fully informed as to the original environmental conditions of the individual species, for these condition their physiology and in particular the induction of the inflorescence. So a period of relative cold (as, for example, during the Philippines winter) is vitally important for the 'programming' of a potential inflorescence which will develop during the following spring. Obviously it is not so much the absolute temperatures as the annual temperature variations that are the determining factors in this process. Consequently, in order to induce an inflorescence on a *Phalaenopsis* grown as a house plant, the answer is to provide it, for several weeks, with a day temperature of 61°F (16°C) and a night temperature of 55°F (13°C).

Because *Phalaenopsis* have roots that are fragile, invasive and liable to adhere to nearby surfaces, it is not a good idea to move them around once an ideal position has been found.

■ Humidity and watering
These orchids suffer considerably from prolonged drought and consequently need regular watering. The intervals will

Phalaenopsis cornu-cervi. The special colour and texture of the flower have encouraged growers to use it widely for hybridization.

Phalaenopsis Rousserole 'Françoise Lecoufle', AM/RHS. This magnificent hybrid was created by the firm of Vacherot et Lecoufle in 1983.

Phalaenopsis
Blume

Tribe: Vandeae
Subtribe: Sarcanthinae

depend on circumstances, but some basic rules can be set:

- water weekly during the growth period;
- water every 10–15 days during the winter;
- water *Phalaenopsis* in hanging baskets every four days.

One essential precaution must be to avoid soaking the base of the leaves where water tends to collect because of their sheath-like form. Stagnating water will sometimes cause the leaves to rot. To prevent this happening (which need not mean the death of the plant), water *Phalaenopsis* in the morning.

A high level of surrounding humidity always does the plants good, especially when the temperature is raised, and this may be done in two ways:

- in the greenhouse, by regular damping down of the ground and by growing shade plants under the staging;
- indoors, by placing the pots in a container of gravel, half-filled with water. In comparison with water on its own, the gravel increases the surface of evaporation and raises the surrounding moisture level more rapidly.

■ Compost
Phalaenopsis are usually grown in pine bark (about $\frac{1}{2}$ in/1 cm pieces but varying from $\frac{1}{4}$ to $\frac{3}{4}$ in/0.5 to 1.5 cm according to the size of the plant). Some growers add variable quantities of polyurethane moss, peat fibre and/or charcoal.

In fact, all these compositions suit the plants quite well, the most important point being the anchorage of the roots in the bark fragments or large particles of the chosen compost.

Doritis pulcherrima. This plant, originally from China, Burma and Indonesia, comes in a number of varieties. Hybridized with *Phalaenopsis*, it brings to them its purple colour and firmer texture.

Phalaenopsis schilleriana. Reichenbach gave it this name in 1860 in tribute to Consul Schiller, who discovered the species in 1858 (*below, left*).

Phalaenopsis equestris. This species, growing widely in all the Philippine islands, is found from sea level to a height of about 1000 ft (300 m).

When cultivating the plants in hanging baskets, it is a good idea to add a little sphagnum moss to the mixture so as to reduce loss of water through evaporation.

■ Repotting

Phalaenopsis are monopodial plants. Unlike sympodial genera with rhizomes (such as *Cattleya*), they do not need frequent repotting. The operation causes too much trauma because the roots are so fragile and tend to stick to the sides of the pot, and must therefore be approached with great care. Even so, there are certain symptoms which may leave no alternative but to repot urgently: a plant that is too cramped; alteration or break-up of the compost; poor appearance of the roots; accidental excess of salinity (either by omitting to rinse the compost prior to feeding, or not rinsing it thoroughly).

Depending on the signs, repotting can be done at intervals of six months (young plants) or two years. Common sense and intuition are the most reliable guidelines as to the right moment for carrying it out. Some growers prefer to repot in summer, after normal flowering, when development of the plant shoots is at its peak; others choose spring or early summer (when plant growth resumes).

■ Ailments to which *Phalaenopsis* are prone

***Bacterial attack due to* Erwinia cypripedii** The sign of this disease is the appearance of blisters on the leaf, soon followed by soft rotting. The remedy is to make a broad cut beneath the affected part, taking all the necessary aseptic precautions, then to apply a little copper based fungicide powder to the wound. To prevent the disease spreading further, lower the temperature slightly so as to diminish relative humidity.

Necrosis of the central leaves This is due to the stagnation of water in the base of the sheathing leaves. Cut away the diseased parts and wait until an underlying bud generates a new shoot.

Rotting of the neck The base of the leaf turns red because of a *Sclerotina* type fungus. This is a contagious disease. Cut away the affected parts, paint with fungicide and isolate the plant carefully (again follow the rules of Walter Bertsch).

Pleione

David Don

Tribe: Coelogyneae   Subtribe: Coelogyninae

The name *Pleione* is derived from that of a character in Greek mythology: the mother of the Pleiades. The genus was first described and named in 1825 by the English botanist David Don in his monograph on the flora of Nepal. Today it comprises ten or so species, epiphytes or lithophytes, widely distributed around the Himalayas, in northern India, Burma, southern China, Thailand and Laos. They are orchids which grow at altitudes of 3300–10,000 ft (1000–3300 m).

Sympodial plants with pseudobulbs and deciduous leaves, *Pleione* should be cultivated in the cool house with an absolute winter rest period. Provided certain precautions are taken, it is possible, in temperate regions, to grow them as hardy subjects, especially as part of the rock garden.

■ Light
Pleione require moderate shading while they are growing. If grown outdoors, never expose them fully to the sun.

■ Temperature
These orchids can stand very low winter temperatures. When grown outside, they will eventually need to be covered by straw so as to prevent their temperature dropping below 32°F (0°C). In the greenhouse, they need to be placed in the coolest section at 41–44°F (5–7°C). In summer, they should be kept, as far as possible, under 77°F (25°C). Any method for keeping them cool – shading, spraying and ventilation – is acceptable.

■ Humidity and watering
Watering should only begin in the spring when the first roots appear. It should be done sparingly, especially in this initial phase. A good humidity level should be maintained.

During growth, watering can be more generous and may be alternated daily with spraying of the compost.

As winter approaches, watering should be more spaced out, then completely suspended when the leaves fall. The plant must then be placed in a cool, dry spot.

■ Feeding
The classic pattern applies here: a fertilizer rich in phosphate when the vegetative cycle commences, followed by one richer in nitrogen and potassium after flowering and until the rest period.

Pleione limprichtii. Pleione are epiphytic plants even though many of their characteristics are typical of terrestrial orchids.

Repotting and compost

Should it become necessary, repotting may be done in early spring. A mixture recommended by Georges Morel, a great collector of *Pleione* orchids, is made up of 30 per cent osmunda root, 30 per cent sphagnum moss, 30 per cent leaf mould and 10 per cent sand and garden soil.

Many growers use heavier composts, such as one composed of peat, leaf mould, sand and fresh soil.

Naturally, when growing the plants outside, the soil must be prepared with this type of compost, with pebbles at the bottom of the hole for drainage and a film of plastic around the sides of the hole.

When repotting, it is possible to divide the clumps. The pseudobulbs should then be arranged so that their bases are just buried in the compost.

small plants, 6–8 in (15–20 cm)	plants for the cool house, but can be grown outdoors in temperate regions
extreme temperatures: 32°F (0°C) in winter; 77–79°F (25–26°C) in summer	
absolute rest period in winter	spring flowering

Pleione formosana. As its name indicates, Formosa (Taiwan) is its country of origin but it is also found in northern China, in variable forms and colours.

Restrepia Humboldt, Bonpland and Kunth
Pleurothallis Robert Brown

Tribe: Epidendreae   Subtribe: Pleurothallidinae

Only quite recently was the genus *Restrepia* separated botanically from the genus *Pleurothallis*. In fact, the plants of both genera are very closely related, their habits and methods of cultivation being identical. There are some thirty species of *Restrepia* and about a thousand of *Pleurothallis*, which makes the latter genus the largest in South America and the second largest worldwide after *Bulbophyllum*.

The distribution range of these orchids in vast (Venezuela, Mexico, Panama, Ecuador and Colombia). They are, for the most part, plants originally from the medium- and high-altitude, misty, wet tropical forests; so they need to be cultivated in the cool greenhouse. It is worth noting, however, that certain species of *Pleurothallis* have adapted to much warmer conditions – hardly surprising for such an enormous genus. So there are many exceptions to the rule.

The majority of *Pleurothallis* are of little horticultural interest, for their flowers are few and nondescript. But some species are supremely elegant, and such plants are both rare and highly prized by collectors. They are of great botanical interest, if only for the opportunity they provide to study the differentiation and evolution of this much diversified genus.

In contrast, the *Restrepia* species are natural gems, with flowers that astonishingly seem to reproduce the glowing forms of the insects which pollinate them. Moreover, so perfect is their appearance that they are treasured by collectors to such an extent that plants of this genus have only very occasionally been used for hybridization.

Restrepia and *Pleurothallis* both exhibit a very curious plant structure: a

Restrepia lansbergii. Originally from Venezuela, *Restrepia* is closely related to *Pleurothallis*, a genus with which it was formerly confused.

slender rhizome from which a number of stems develop, each stem branching out into a fairly coriaceous leaf (cladode) and the axil to which the flowers are attached. There is a single flower in *Restrepia*, but *Pleurothallis* are multiple flowered.

In *Restrepia* the flower structure has evolved in an unmistakable manner:

- the two lower sepals have fused to form a lip;
- the upper sepal has adopted a translucent, insect-shaped appearance;
- the lip itself has retreated deep inside the flower.

■ Light

In the context of their rain forest habitat, *Restrepia* and *Pleurothallis* orchids need to be cultivated in moderate, subdued light.

cool temperatures under 64°F (18°C)	
constantly moist compost	high surrounding humidity (70–80 per cent)
moderate lighting	good ventilation
apply a balanced feed throughout year	not to be cultivated indoors

Restrepia elegans (detail of flower). It was discovered in Venezuela around 1846. Its insect-like appearance would appear to play a major role in its pollination.

Restrepia
Humboldt, Bonpland
and
Kunth
Pleurothallis
Robert Brown

Tribe: Epidendreae
Subtribe: Pleurothallidinae

■ Temperature

Night: 53–59°F (12–15°C). Day: under 64°F (18°C), for the greater part of the year.

Restrepia species can withstand rather higher daytime temperatures (up to 79°F/26°C) for short periods, provided that at night temperatures are reduced to around 61–64°F (16–18°C).

It is possible to grow these orchids in the coolest part of an intermediate house; but they do even better in a cool house. In northern Europe and other cool temperate regions, provided certain precautions are taken, they can even be grown in a greenhouse which is not air-conditioned.

■ Humidity and watering

The compost must be kept constantly damp, but not saturated. In summer, naturally, watering will be more frequent. The plants can even be given a daily spraying so that the surface of the compost is wettened on days when they are not watered.

This need to ensure that the compost is always moist but never soaked demands a good deal of skill and intuition for the real requirements of the plant.

Lacking water storage organs, *Restrepia* and *Pleurothallis* have no rest period, so the level of humidity should be maintained all year round at 70–80 per cent.

■ Feeding

These plants flower for lengthy periods that are not always well defined, so it is difficult to pinpoint a precise vegetative cycle. Feeding can be carried out all year round, using a balanced formula feed twice a month.

Pleurothallis grobyi. This species with tiny flowers (2–3 mm) is found in Mexico, Central America and the northern part of South America.

Pleurothallis species. This
orchid, so far unnamed,
comes from Central America.
The genus *Pleurothallis*
comprises, according to
estimates, 900–1000 species.

■ Ventilation

Special attention must be given to this
vitally important point. Taking into consideration the high local and surrounding
humidity that plants of both these genera
enjoy, good ventilation remains the best
safeguard against bacterial and fungal
infections.

■ Repotting and compost

The necessity for effective drainage and
constant humidity imposes the use of small
plastic pots. Both *Restrepia* and *Pleurothallis*
were traditionally grown in a compost
consisting mainly of finely chopped
osmunda fibre; but the rapid disintegra-
tion of this medium entailed annual repotting, which puts stress on the plants. This
led growers to seek other formulae, notably a mixture in equal parts of small-
grained terracotta, pine bark and washed
aquarium gravel. This type of compost
usually lasts about three years. The
slightest sign of trouble, in the form of
stunted shoots or sickly leaves, means that
repotting should proceed without delay.

If the roots show symptoms of necrosis,
a new root shoot may be induced by temporarily repotting the plant in fresh
sphagnum moss (as for *Masdevallia*).

■ Propagation

It is not a good idea to divide a clump at
the time of repotting for this constitutes a
major trauma for the plant and spoils its
whole appearance. *Restrepia* and *Pleurothallis* both have the peculiarity – rare in
the orchid world – of reproducing themselves by simple cuttings. All that needs to
be done, is to take, after flowering, a stem
and its leaf and to place the former in
moist compost (of the same type used for
the adult plant), giving the leaf fresh air,
just touching the surface of the compost.
In these conditions the bud that appears
at the junction of the stem and the cladode
will develop into an adult plant, coming
into flower two or three years later.

Stanhopea Hooker and GONGORINAE

Tribe: Cymbidieae   **Subtribe: Stanhopeinae**

In 1829 Sir William Hooker described and named the genus *Stanhopea* as a tribute to Philip Stanhope, president of the London Medico-Botanical Society. The genus nowadays contains twenty-five species, fairly widely distributed through North, Central and South America. These plants, together with those of the genera *Acineta, Gongora, Coryanthes* and *Peristeria*, form part of the subtribe Stanhopeinae, orchids that can all be cultivated identically, under the same temperature conditions.

Stanhopea produce flowers that are so strange in form that it is sometimes hard to realize they are orchids. The flower spike grows downward and as the flowers open they given out a heady, pungent scent of chocolate which, once experienced, is never forgotten. This perfume attracts pollinating insects, notably bees of the genus *Euglossa*, from afar. The specific attraction is quite remarkable, for each species of *Stanhopea* is visited by one, sometimes two, species of bee, to the exclusion of all others, even when there may be fifty or more species in the area (cf. the works and observations of Dressler). Having identified the source of this perfume, the bee ventures inside the flower, irresistibly drawn towards the strong-smelling secretion. So powerful is the scent that it completely stupefies the bee which, as if intoxicated or drugged, tumbles backwards or sideways, invariably ending up among the folds of the toboggan-shaped lip. From here the bee is pas-sively conveyed along the guidelines of the lip to the tip of the column and into contact with the pollinia. Recovering its senses, the pollinia sticking to its back, the bee now goes through the same rigmarole inside another flower, suffers the same indignities and is conducted once more to the column tip. This time, however, it deposits the pollinia of the first flower on the stigma of the second, performing an identical movement in exactly the same spot, so that the new pollinia stick to its back and it is ready to fly off again to fertilize yet another flower.

Many of the Gongorinae thus exhibit a remarkable combination of visual, structural and chemical mechanisms which complement the nervous reactions of the insect. Indeed, these orchids seem to have built into their structure not only the motivations but also the chance effects of animal behaviour. What Darwin had sensed when he first saw the *Angraecum* spur, recognizing its implications, surely reaches a peak of sophistication here.

The fascination of a *Stanhopea* may well be associated with its tropical origins, but in an even more subtle fashion it may induce a sense of wonder that here we have a living mechanism which bears witness to an evolutionary process that still remains a total mystery.

Stanhopea flower at different times, according to species, but perhaps most frequently in early summer. Each flower only lasts about four days.

The plants are sympodial with quite small, ovoid pseudobulbs that bear a single large, crinkled leaf on a fairly long stalk. The leaves are persistent. The inflorescence grows from the base of the main pseudobulb and, curiously, points downwards. In its natural habitat it emerges from the adjacent tangle of roots and pseudobulbs to develop freely in mid-air, just beneath the branch supporting the plant.

It is obviously impossible to cultivate *Stanhopea* in ordinary pots where the flower spike would develop inside the compost without finding any way out, except perhaps through the drainage hole. So they have to be grown in hanging baskets, in which situation they present few cultural problems.

■ Light

Stanhopea appreciate moderate shading.

■ Temperature

Intermediate house temperatures suit them well. The majority of *Stanhopea* are tropical orchids from altitudes ranging from 3300 to 9000 ft (1000–2700 m). Those from the highest regions can be raised in the cool house, close to the glass.

To ensure balanced growth, make sure that there is a marked difference between day/night and seasonal temperatures. The best solution is to keep them in the intermediate house in summer and move them to the cool house in winter. Do not put them outside during the summer.

■ Humidity and watering

These orchids require a high humidity level and copious watering during the stage of vegetative growth, accompanied by good ventilation. The rhythm of watering should be reduced in autumn, and a total rest period observed during winter in the cool house. At that time the plants may be lightly watered occasionally to prevent the compost becoming too dry and the pseudobulbs shrivelling.

■ Feeding

A normal or half-dose of 20-20-20 fertilizer should be applied monthly during the entire active growth stage. Feeding is then suspended, along with watering, in the autumn.

■ Repotting and compost

Stanhopea are cultivated either in hanging baskets or in suspended containers, suitably perforated. Slatted wooden or wickerwork hanging baskets are the types most frequently used. However, they have the disadvantage of encouraging the compost to dry out too rapidly, which often leads to the production of smaller flowers.

The compost used is that generally employed for *Cattleya*: 40 per cent pine bark, 20 per cent peat, 10 per cent polyurethane moss, 20 per cent expanded polystyrene, 10 per cent expanded clay and an addition of dolomite lime at the rate of 3 g per litre.

reputedly easy to grow in an intermediate greenhouse	cultivation in hanging containers
moderate lighting	variable flowering period, of short duration
repot every three years in spring	propagate by clump division

Stanhopea bucephalus (syn. *Stanhopea oculata*). Originally from Central America, the *stanhopea* are called 'bull's head' by the Indians. Lindley probably borrowed the allusion when naming this species.

Vanda

Jones

Tribe: Vandeae   Subtribe: Sarcanthinae

The origin of the generic name is the Sanskrit word for the species known as *Vanda tessellata*. Originally from tropical Asia, the sixty or so species that belong to the genus have a vast distribution that covers India, South-east Asia, New Guinea, the Solomon Islands, northern Australia and the Philippines.

Vanda are epiphytic or lithophytic plants, monopodial in habit, of very variable size, ranging from 8 in to $6\frac{1}{2}$ ft (0.20–2 m), and divided into two categories: those with flat leaves and those with cylindrical leaves (such as *Vanda teres*). Species of the latter group are adapted to heat and full sun; those with flat or ribbon leaves do better in a shaded position. Some of them (like *Vanda coerulea*) are high-altitude plants which need to be cultivated in the cool or intermediate house. Others, adapted to the humid lowlands of tropical Asia, do best in the warm house. Because of such varied needs, cultural guidelines for *Vanda* are somewhat complicated.

These orchids have been widely hybridized both with one another and with related genera, including *Phalaenopsis, Renanthera, Arachnis, Ascocentrum, Aerides* and *Vandopsis*. The plants thus obtained, often extremely beautiful, bear composite names such as *Renantanda, Aranda, Ascocenda, Aeridovanda*, etc. Many of them can be cultivated in the intermediate greenhouse.

The subtribe Sarcanthinae, to which the *Vanda* belong, contains a large number of genera which are capable of fertilizing one another, which explains why growers have been

Vanda Tan Chin Tuan. This is a hybrid (*Vanda dearei* × Josephine van Brero), much appreciated for its harmony and glowing colours.

successful in producing so many hybrids since the end of the nineteenth century.

Many *Vanda* grow to a considerable size and for this reason can only be cultivated in a greenhouse of sufficient height.

■ Light

The cylindrical-leaved *Vanda* need plenty of light and can stand direct sun provided they are not exposed to it too suddenly; they need a period of adaptation. Bright light, in fact, is essential for these plants if they are to flower well. Should it be impossible to provide such conditions (as may be the case in northern Europe), it is better not to try cultivating them.

The flat-leaved *Vanda* are far less demanding as far as light is concerned. They cannot tolerate direct sun and need to be shaded (50–60 per cent) during the summer.

■ Temperature

The following distinctions have to be made:

- *Vanda* with cylindrical leaves require warm house conditions: a minimum temperature of 61–63°F (16–17°C) at night during the winter and a maximum of 86–90°F (30–32°C) in the summer. A daytime temperature of 80°F (27°C) suits them very well;
- some *Vanda* with flat leaves are adapted to warm house conditions but can get by with somewhat lower temperatures;
- the flat-leaved *Vanda* suited to the cool or intermediate greenhouse need a winter night temperature of about 50–54°F (10–12°C) and a summer daytime temperature of 72–75°F (22–24°C).

In general, *Vanda* require day and night temperatures that differ by 9–11°F (5–6°C).

monopodial plants which can grow to a considerable height	simple reproduction by pollarding or by repotting cuttings of shoots
varying needs for light, water and heat justify separation into three horticultural groups	plants reputedly difficult to cultivate in temperate regions, but quite easy in a warm Mediterranean climate and even more so in the tropics (see table below)

Vanda	Greenhouse	Watering	Light	Culture in temperate climate	Culture in tropical climate
flat-leaved	warm	no winter rest period (with exceptions)	moderate lighting	quite easy	very easy
flat-leaved	intermediate or cool	partial rest in winter; restrict watering	moderate lighting	difficult, though possible	easy
cylindrical-leaved	warm	no winter rest period	plenty of bright light	very difficult	very easy

Arachnis flos-aëris. This is one of the rare orchids described by Linnaeus in 1753 in his *Species Plantarum*. It is found over much of South-east Asia.

Vanda
Jones

Tribe: Vandeae
Subtribe: Sarcanthinae

Renanthera imschootiana.
Originating in Assam, Laos and Vietnam, it was first flowered by a Belgian collector, M. A. Imschoot, and described in 1891.

Vanda coerulea. This mountain plant grows at 2700–5500 ft (800–1700 m) over a vast area which includes the Himalayan foothills, Burma and Thailand (*below*).

■ Humidity and watering

It is essential that while they are actively growing, i.e. from early spring to late autumn, *Vanda* should enjoy a high level of humidity and be watered frequently. When it is very hot, watering should be supplemented by daily spraying of the compost. Winter is a relative rest period for the plants, and although watering should not be suspended, it must be spaced at longer intervals.

After flowering and then for about a fortnight, it is advisable to rest the plants and stop watering, except for occasional light spraying of the compost.

■ Feeding

Most growers are content to give *Vanda* a 10-10-10 fertilizer twice a month in the course of vegetative growth, except, of course, during the brief rest period after flowering.

■ Compost

Vanda are strongly epiphytic plants which are not greatly dependent upon the nature of their compost, and this explains why growers have such a wide variety of options in this respect. In the tropics they can be raised on large slabs of tree fern where they readily adopt a liana-like habit. In the greenhouse, certain species will do perfectly well in a simple wooden hanging basket with slats through which their roots can coil (without any compost inside).

When *Vanda* are grown in pots, the compost can be quite simple, such as charcoal. Pine bark is equally satisfactory, with an addition of varying amounts of charcoal, brick or polystyrene.

Renanthera storiei × *Ascocenda*
Peggy Foo. This recent
trigeneric hybrid has
Renanthera, Ascocentrum and
Vanda in its parentage. The
slow growth of *Vanda,*
however, has greatly
restricted its hybridization.

■ Repotting

Vanda do not enjoy being repotted. This is
why the operation should be carried out
only once every three or four years. The
best time to do this is when plant growth
resumes at the end of winter.

Apart from obvious deterioration of the
compost, one sign that repotting is necessary is necrosis of the lower part of the
plant and the consequent withering of
older leaves. This means cutting away the
entire lower section. Sometimes the roots
will have adhered too tightly to the sides of
the pot, in which case they may need to be
broken. But since this will injure or
damage them, complete resection is the
best solution, keeping the underlying roots
intact.

The repotting operation can be made
easier by soaking the roots, which are often
very tough, in water at a temperature of
86°F (30°C) so as to soften them up for
correct positioning. Stem and roots should
then be buried shallowly in the compost,
and the plant supported by a suitable
stake.

Pots must allow adequate drainage and
aeration. Rather than plastic pots, therefore, use earthenware pots with broad side
openings.

With *Vanda*, comparatively few precautions need to be taken after repotting.
Watering may be quickly resumed, provided the section of the stem has been
correctly cauterized.

■ Propagation

This can be done simply by cuttings of the
shoots, provided with roots, that appear
from time to time on the main stem, or
even by a cutting of the entire upper part
of the stem.

Unlike the keikis produced by *Dendrobium*, which are often a sign that the plant
is in poor condition, the shoots thrown out
by *Vanda* are wholly physiological.

Zygopetalum

Hooker

Tribe: Maxillarieae   Subtribe: Zygopetalinae

Sir William Hooker described this genus for the first time in 1827 and gave it this name with reference to the shape of the lip, the basal part of which is very swollen so as to resemble a yoke that links together the two petals (from Greek *zygon* = yoke and *petalon* = petal).

There are eighteen species of *Zygopetalum*, most of them being terrestrial and a few epiphytic. Their area of distribution covers the entire northern part of South America and Central America. The majority of species occur in Brazil.

As a rule these plants grow at high altitude and must therefore be cultivated in the intermediate house.

The *Zygopetalum* orchids have pseudobulbs of varying dimensions, some large, others almost non-existent, with 2–5 long, narrow leaves (of about 18 in/45 cm) at the top, which are persistent, falling after two or three years. The large inflorescence, measuring 2–3 ft (0.60–1 m), develops from the new leaf shoot at the base of the previous year's pseudobulb. The various species flower at different times of the year, for as long as a month or thereabouts. The flowers have an extraordinary scent which some compare to that of a narcissus.

Growers have successfully hybridized *Zygopetalum* species with one another and with related genera (*Chondrorhyncha, Batemannia, Lycaste, Colax, Zygonisia, Promenaea*, etc.), but the full potentialities of the genus in this context are still to be fully explored.

■ **Light**

Zygopetalum need fairly bright light (moderate shading). Full sun is harmful to them.

■ **Temperature**

Normal intermediate house temperatures suit them best: a minimum in winter of 53–57°F (12–14°C) and a maximum in summer of 75–79°F (24–26°C).

■ **Humidity and watering**

During the vegetative growth phase watering should be abundant and regular. Since the pots are fairly big and the compost retains moisture well, this means a good watering about once a week. The new shoots are extremely sensitive to excessive humidity or to any water collecting among the leaves and likely to cause rotting. On no account should the leaves be sprayed, as this may mark them.

When the plant has finished growing, towards the end of summer, it will need a period of several weeks' rest, and at that time it is only necessary to spray the compost so that it does not dry out too much; normal watering can then be resumed, though with longer intervals until growth begins again.

Zygopetalum B. G. White 'Stonehurst' AM-HCC/AOS. This is one of the most beautiful contemporary hybrids of the genus.

The bigger the pseudobulbs, the longer the rest period. In the plant's original habitat, this is the season of relative or absolute drought, a condition essential for inducing the inflorescence.

Optimal surrounding humidity, depending on the time of year, ranges from 40 to 60 per cent.

■ Repotting and compost

Terrestrial *Zygopetalum* species are grown in a fairly heavy compost, consisting perhaps of 2 parts peat, 2 parts sand, 1 part vermiculite and 1 part fine-grained pine bark.

An alternative to this is a mixture of 2 parts peat, 5 parts pine bark, 1 part polyurethane moss, 1 part expanded polystyrene and dolomite lime at the rate of 3 g per litre.

Epiphytic *Zygopetalum* do best in a lighter compost, similar to that used for *Cattleya*. This might be made up of 50 per cent pine bark, 15 per cent polyurethane, 15 per cent expanded polystyrene, 20 per cent tree fern and dolomite lime at 3 g per litre.

Pots should preferably be of plastic and big enough to allow the roots to spread out freely. The roots, in fact, grow rapidly but they are quite delicate and do not lend themselves readily to repotting. This operation can be carried out every other year, ideally during the late summer rest period, as this will offer them perfect conditions for recovery and regrowth.

■ Propagation

The simplest method is by clump division at the time of repotting; but it does not have to be done automatically.

■ Ailments

If the atmosphere in summer is too dry, there is a strong risk of the leaves succumbing to attacks by mites.

intermediate greenhouse plants	variable compost, depending on habit
large size: about 2 ft (60 cm)	need bright light but not direct sun
long flowering period, scented flowers	rest period of several weeks in late summer
repot every two years in late summer, in fairly big pots	genus quite difficult to cultivate

Zygopetalum Clayii. There are eighteen or so species of *Zygopetalum*, most of them from Brazil, particularly the Amazon basin. This is a hybrid between *Z. mackayi* and *Z. maxillare*.

Glossary

Acaulous Without a stem.

Actinomorphic Radially symmetrical and therefore capable of being divided vertically into symmetrical halves.

Albumen Reserve tissues of seed, designed to feed the embryo in the course of germination.

Anther Thickened tip of the stamen which contains the pollen.

Apex Tip of a shoot, stem, pseudobulb, etc.

Asymbiotic Form of culture not requiring stimulation of growth by use of fungi.

Axil Angle between upper side of a leaf and bulb or leaf and stem.

Back-bulb Pseudobulb on certain orchids used for propagation.

Bilateral Relating to either side of a central area: two-sided.

Bract Modified leaf enfolding the base of an inflorescence or flower.

Carpel One of the elements, of which there are three in orchids, that form the flower's female sexual organ.

Chlorophyll Green colouring matter of leaves and plants, essential for photosynthesis.

Chlorosis Loss of green colour in leaves, due to unsuitable conditions, poor light, shortage of nutritive substances, parasite attack, etc.

Cladode Leaf-like flattened branch or stem.

Column Central sexual structure of the orchid flower, consisting of stamens and style.

Compost Soil or growing mixture for rooting, made up of fibre, moss, bark, loam, etc. in varying proportions.

Coriaceous Thick, leathery.

Corolla Ring of petals protecting the flower's reproductive organs.

Cultivar Horticulturally produced variety of plant.

Deciduous Shedding leaves annually.

Dehiscence Natural splitting open, when ripe, of a fruit, capsule, anther, etc. to release contents.

Entomophilous Plant pollinated by insects.

Epiphyte Plant that lives above ground on another plant, not as a parasite but for purposes of support, deriving nutrition from the air.

Family Wide group of plants which contains a number of genera.

Fungus Plant organism without chlorophyll which derives sustenance from other plants (or animals), causing various ailments.

Fusiform Spindle-shaped; tapering towards either end.

Genus Subdivision of family, a group of closely related plant species, indicated by first word of the scientific name.

Germination Sprouting of seed to form a shoot and produce a new plant.

Grex Group of plants (specifically orchids) obtained from a crossing of particular parents, capable of displaying variations as a result of different genetic combinations.

Habit Characteristic outward appearance or bearing of a plant (e.g. terrestrial or epiphytic).

Habitat Area or region where a plant naturally lives.

Hybrid Plant created by artificially crossing two species of the same genus or of related genera.

Hygrometer Instrument for measuring atmospheric humidity level.

Inflorescence Part of a plant that bears flowers, which are variously arranged on the axis to form spikes, racemes, panicles, etc.

Internode Part of a stem between two nodes or joints.

Keiki Young orchid plantlet developing from the stem, used for propagating certain species.

Labellum (or lip) Lowermost petal of flower, in orchids often brightly coloured and originally shaped to attract pollinating insects.

Lateral Positioned at the side, as of a branch, shoot or leaf.

Liana Climbing or twining tropical plant.

Lithophyte Plant that grows on the surface of rocks.

Meristem Formative plant tissue consisting of undifferentiated cells which evolve into differentiated plant tissues and organs.

Micro-organism Microscopic organism, some species of which supply nutrition to the plant by decomposing the ingredients of the substrate.

Monopodial Orchid plant, growing from the terminal shoot, which has neither rhizome nor pseudobulbs.

Morphogenesis Collective processes which determine the form and structure of organisms.

Mycelium Vegetative part of a fungus.

Osmunda Type of fern, the roots of which are used as an ingredient for orchid composts.

Ovary Enlarged lower part of the carpel where the seed is formed.

Ovoid Oval, egg-shaped.

Parasite Animal or plant living at the expense of another organism, drawing nutriment directly from it.

Pendulous Hanging down loosely, as of an inflorescence.

Perianth Outer part of the flower, comprising the sepals and petals, enclosing the essential organs.

Persistent Leaves that remain on the plant for more than one growing season.

Petal Modified leaf, usually brightly coloured, forming part of the corolla.

pH Scale, from 0 to 14, for measuring the acidity or alkalinity of the soil.

Photosynthesis In plants, the conversion of atmospheric carbon dioxide and water into carbohydrates as a result of exposure to light.

Pistil Female reproductive parts of flower, consisting of ovary, style and stigma.

Plantlet   Embryonic or rudimentary plant.
Pollinia   Hardened, cohesive mass of pollen grains, characteristic of orchids.
Protocorm   Intermediate vegetative stage between embryo and plantule, characteristic of orchids.
Pseudobulb   False bulb; swollen stem of an orchid, transformed into a storage organ, bearing leaves and flowers.

Ramified   Branched.
Receptacle   Modified part of an axis which bears the organs of a flower or of an inflorescence.
Repotting   Procedure carried out annually or at longer intervals, usually at the end of the growth cycle, whereby a plant is lifted and replanted in fresh soil or compost, often in a bigger container, to provide more space for the roots.
Resupination   Rotating 180° movement of the ovary which in orchids brings the lip into an upside-down position when the flower opens.
Rhizome   Modified horizontal stem, usually underground and acting as a storage organ, which bears roots, leaves and flowering stems.
Rostellum   One of three fused stigmas situated between the anther and the stigmatic cavity, designed to prevent self-fertilization.

Sheath   Basal portion of a leaf, enfolding the stalk.
Species   Group of related plants belonging to a genus, indicated by second word of the scientific name.

Sphagnum   Type of moss used as an ingredient for orchid compost.
Stamen   Male reproductive organ of flower, consisting of the filament and the anther, containing pollen.
Stigma   Enlarged terminal part of the pistil, generally sticky, where pollen is deposited.
Style   Elongated part of the pistil between the ovary and the stigma.
Substrate   Growing medium; compost.
Symbiotic   Two or more organisms living in association, usually for their mutual benefit.
Sympodial   Orchid plant, growing from an axillary shoot, possessing a rhizome and pseudobulbs.

Taxon   Any group, such as family, tribe, genus, species, etc. used in plant or animal classification (taxonomy).
Terrestrial   Growing in the ground, as distinct from epiphytic or lithophytic.
Transpiration   Exhalation of watery vapour from the surface of leaves or other parts of a plant.

Variety   Subdivision of a species, indicated by third word of the scientific name.
Velamen   Spongy tissue surrounding the roots.
Virus   Infective agent responsible for causing various plant diseases.

Zygomorphic   Capable of being divided longitudinally into symmetrical halves.

Orchid Societies

United Kingdom

The Orchid Society of Great Britain
120 Crofton Road
Orpington
Kent BR6 8HZ

The British Orchid Council
20 Newbury Drive
Davyhulme
Manchester M31 2FA

United States of America

American Orchid Society
6000 South Olive Avenue
West Palm Beach
Florida 33405

The Cymbidium Society of America
6881 Wheeler Avenue
Westminster
California 92683

Acknowledgements

The authors would like to thank the following for their help in the preparation of this book:

Mme Geneviève Bert; M. and Mme Gaston Chatel; Mlle Marie Cote; M. Yves Delange; Mme Monique Ducreux; M. Jean-Yves Gil; M. Georges Herbert; M. Pierre Jacquet; Mlle Armelle Joly; M. and Mme Maurice Lecoufle; M. and Mme Marcel Lecoufle; M. and Mme Philippe Lecoufle; M. Yves Laissus; M. Jacques Metron (*in memoriam*); M. Jean-François Muller; Mme Odile Roche; M. Patrick Lafaite.

Thanks also go to the personnel at the Établissements Vacherot et Lecoufle and Marcel Lecoufle. Finally, the authors are especially grateful to Mme Djouher Si Ahmed for all the help and encouragement she has given them on this book.

Bibliography

ARDITTI, J.

Orchid Biology: Reviews and Perspectives, Cornell University Press, New York and London, 1977

BECHTEL, H., CRIBB, P., and LAUNERT, E.

The Manual of Cultivated Orchid Species, Blandford, London, 3rd. ed. 1991

BLACK, Peter McKenzie

The Complete Book of Orchid Growing, Ward Lock, London, 2nd. ed. 1988

BRISTOW, Alec

Orchids. A Wisley Handbook, Cassell/The Royal Horticultural Society, London, 3rd. ed. 1991

DARWIN, C.

The Various Contrivances by which Orchids are Fertilized by Insects, John Murray, London, 1862

DRESSLER, R. L.

The Orchids: Natural History and Classification, Harvard University Press, Cambridge, Mass., and London, 1981

HAWKES, A. D.

Encyclopedia of Cultivated Orchids, Faber and Faber, London, 1965

JAMES, I. D.

The Orchid Grower's Handbook, Blandford, London, 1988

LEIGH, David

Orchids Their Care and Cultivation, Cassell, London, 1990

NORTHEN, R. T.

Home Orchid Growing, Van Nostrand Reinhold, New York, 1970

RITTERSHAUSEN, B. & W.

Orchid Growing Illustrated, Blandford, London, 1979

RITTERSHAUSEN, B. & W.

Orchids in Colour, Blandford, London, 1979

SANDER, David

Orchids and their Cultivation, Blandford, London, 1932

SWINSON, A.

Frederick Sander: The Orchid King, Hodder and Stoughton, London, 1970

WILLIAMS, B. S.

Orchid Growers' Manual, Wheldon & Wesley, Herts, 1894

WITHNER, C. L.

The Orchids: Scientific Studies, Wiley, New York and London, 1974

Index

Page numbers in *italic* refer to illustrations